COLLECTING
PAPER MONEY AND
BONDS

Collecting
Paper Money and
Bonds

COLIN NARBETH

ROBIN HENDY

CHRISTOPHER STOCKER

STUDIO VISTA

IN ASSOCIATION WITH STANLEY GIBBONS

A Studio Vista book published by
Cassell Ltd.
35 Red Lion Square, London WC1R 4SG
and at Sydney, Auckland, Toronto,
Johannesburg,
an affiliate of
Macmillan Publishing Co. Inc.,
New York

Text and illustrations © C. Narbeth and
R. Hendy 1979
Design Joop de Nijs gvn
Created by Meijer Pers bv,
Amsterdam, The Netherlands

First published 1979

ISBN 0 289 70880 X

Printed and bound in Italy by Amilcare Pizzi s.p.a.,
Cinisello Balsamo (Milano).

Contents

1   Collecting paper money and bonds   7

2   The evolution of paper money and the rise
of banking   13

3   The art of banknotes   29

4   Autographed banknotes   45

5   Getting to know old bonds and shares   57

6   Collectors' favourite bonds   79

7   Bonds and shares with an outstanding history   101

Guide to prices   116

Dealers, auction houses, clubs and magazines
specialising in banknotes and bonds   117

1 Collecting Paper Money and Bonds

Bonds, banknotes and cheques are all paper money and, as far as collectors are concerned, form main areas for collecting. So under the title of 'Bonds' the collector embraces share certificates – in fact a much wider field than bonds; banknotes to a collector are not just the notes issued by banks, but an enormous area of unofficial and official scrip – for example, emergency notes issued under duress by a regiment of soldiers cut off from its pay corps, its notes having no more authority than the signature of the officer responsible (such as the Uppington Border Scouts in the Boer war who issued such notes on torn-up strips of khaki shirts). Promissory notes, bills of exchange and sight bills are all studied by banknote collectors. Cheques overlap the world of banknote collecting but, because of their vast number, are often ignored by the banknote collector, and have therefore developed as a field of their own. The essential difference that marks them out from other paper money is that a cheque does not require acceptance. As many tourists have found, even a traveller's cheque is not necessarily accepted.

The intelligent collector has to restrict himself if he intends to develop a collection that records history and tells a comprehensive story of events. Otherwise time alone prohibits him from anything but a very large accumulation. The serious collectors of the world have found that it is necessary to specialise even further. To form a collection of banknotes is a formidable task, but to make such a collection of the notes of one country or one type can be undertaken with a reasonable chance of ending up with a 'completeness' which tells the whole story. Of course, one can never have a 'complete' collection of anything. There is always something that can be added: proofs, specimens, colour trials, original artwork etc. Just how deep specialisation can become is shown by the more established hobbies like philately where many collect just one stamp. An example could be the Penny Black which the collector can be involved with for a lifetime without approaching 'completeness'. Reconstructing eleven plates with 240 stamps to each, the repaired states, the different postmarks and so on, he can only hope to achieve a comprehensive story of that stamp, and, incidentally, amass a small fortune!

The collector is an important person. He contributes to our knowledge of history. Our knowledge of the past is based on the study of items preserved from the past, and is the foundation stone for reaching for further knowledge.

Collectors of paper money very quickly learn the lessons of banking history. Inflation is nothing new, the Mongols had inflation on a scale that makes our present-day difficulties look minor. The collector unravels the reasons and causes in his quest and traces the results. One often wonders if our financial geniuses of modern banking would so readily re-enter the pitfalls of the past if they too were collectors!

It is worth pointing out that the world's great museums would be half empty if it were not for the great collectors of the past who so happily immersed themselves in their hobbies and left the results to their nations so that others might come along and study. For one thing is quite certain, the collector does not own his collection: he is merely a custodian for the short span of a human lifetime. What he does do is preserve the items for the future, whether they be kept intact in a museum or re-circulated to very grateful collectors of a future generation.

This is why the recording of information is so important in the collecting world. At the time of acquisition it may not seem vital that you should record the date, the place and the circumstances but nothing is more fundamental to successful collecting. Memory fades and plays tricks with fact, but a good filing system of well-kept records is invaluable. Just imagine the feelings of an archaeologist who acquires some unique piece of antique pottery from a collector's descendants. If only he could know where it was found he could be on the path of a new chapter of history; but with just the pot to study, the knowledge he can gain is limited.

The problem is that at the time it may not seem important that something should be recorded. But a hundred years from now there may be a dozen reasons which we could never be expected to think of, why detailed information should have been recorded.

Apart from helping to contribute to general knowledge, those collectors who have kept sound records have invariably been delighted in later years – when a record card can jog the memory and bring back happy events of their past.

It would be an impertinence to tell people what to collect or how to collect, but there are some general guidelines which can be given based on the experiences of long-standing collectors.

Apart from all wishing they had kept better records, there are a number of errors made by most collectors when they start. The major error is going for quantity instead of quality.

It is, of course, a natural tendency for a schoolboy to aim at a 'big' collection. It is also a necessary evil in the sense that until the collector has studied the field he cannot get the 'feel' for that particular sector which appeals most to him. But once he has been able to make that decision, quality should become the key word.

Quantity is meaningless in value terms; and many collectors are conscious of their collections being an investment as well as a hobby. How often do the next-of-kin go to a dealer and say they have been left thousands and thousands of something, expecting a respectful and astounded reaction. But the dealer is totally unimpressed, he has heard it all before, and would much rather hear of a small collection with a few crack items in it.

If we take bonds as an example, the pitfall the new collector falls into all too readily is the 'quantity' problem. He sees a set of a particular bond, £5, £10, £20, £50, £100, £500, £1000. Almost invariably there are fewer £1000 bonds issued than any other denomination, and the lower denominations are usually issued in large numbers. He cannot afford the whole set but he finds that for the price of the £1000 bond he can buy the rest of the set, six beautiful items instead of one, for the same money. The authors of this book have done it, our friends have done it, and we have all regretted it. What happens, of course, is that a few years later the collector wants to complete the set. He finds the rare, high-value item has shot up in value out of all proportion to the lower denominations. It is logical, there are fewer of them and more people wanting them. If the collector had settled for the one expensive item at the start, completing the set later is much easier because, as there were far more issued, they are going to be more easily obtained. It is, however, a very hard discipline for a collector to adopt!

Naturally the collector is restricted by his available funds. This, better than anything else, is the spur to making a collector a man of discernment. Faced with a choice the collector has to evaluate and choose. Wealth is always an advantage, but not nearly so important as many would think. Desirable collector's items are not instantly available because someone has produced a cheque book and poised pen. They have to be found first. In many cases they may only come up for sale once in a lifetime; or be buried in a junk shop unrecognised and unappreciated. The collector who knows his subject can recognise such items. It has happened on more than one occasion that a comparatively poor collector has been offered a large sum for an item he acquired through his knowledge for next to nothing. That he sometimes refuses high offers is an insight into the enjoyment and satisfaction that a collector can get from his hobby.

Fair advice to a young collector is never to be put off from collecting something he likes just because of cost. What may be much too expensive at the age of twenty often turns out to be easily afforded in later years; and then the collector wishes he had started at the earlier age even if he could only have bought a handful of items at the beginning. Collecting is not just a matter of acquiring. It is learning, studying, appreciating, and taking advantage of opportunities. Much of this can be achieved by visiting museums, and in talking with fellow collectors.

Collectors are far from being hermits. They have an immediate affinity with anyone else who likes the same subject. They form clubs and societies in order that they can meet fellow collectors and they usually have specialist magazines which publish the latest research findings. Very few of the affairs of man have such a fine and honourable record of non-class- or race-discrimination as that of the collecting world, where a Duke and a dustman can discuss on equal terms quite happily the merits of a collection of rare paper money, and have done.

The new collector should make a point of joining any club or society in his chosen field. Many, who cannot ever expect to attend meetings, will nevertheless join such societies even if only to support them and encourage other people with the same interests.

Books on the subject are invaluable. The first aim of any serious collector is to form a good library. In a few short hours a collector can read and absorb the knowledge of another collector's lifetime experience. Nothing can beat first-hand experience and handling of items, but a library on the subject can prevent a lot of mistakes that other people have made and will pay for its cost over and over again in a collector's lifetime. The true collector is apt to spend more than he can really afford on his hobby. Few ever regret it because if they have collected wisely they have built up an inflation-proof investment. Aware that he is doing this a collector will often spend much more than he would otherwise dream of spending on his hobby. But the five-minute expert who rushes in can easily make a very bad investment. To buy wisely requires an indefinable 'sense' which comes of knowledge, experience and selectivity.

Prime considerations are condition, rarity and demand. If no one else wants an item its value is not affected by its condition or its rarity. Once there is a demand for it the rarity becomes important. If there are only ten items but at least twenty collectors who want them then it follows that only ten can have them. Which ten is decided by how much they will pay. Who those collectors are is then also of importance. If they are all on small incomes there is a limit to the amount they can pay. If, by chance, all twenty are multi-millionaires, then the owner of the item knows he is going to get a very high price.

In practice, most items are available in larger quantities and the demand is spread among all income groups. So the prime consideration becomes condition. In torn and dirty condition a piece of paper money may be quite common, but in absolutely perfect condition we are very likely back to our only ten known. This is more markedly demonstrated in the world of coin collectors than any other, where a coin can be £5 in poor condition and £500 in *fleur de coin* condition. The new collector will quickly appreciate how important it is to define condition accurately.

The collector will soon be bemused by some condition descriptions such as 'brilliant gem FDC', and 'nearly unique' for a rarity description! FDC is the top numismatic condition; other words are superfluous and show the collector the dealer in question does not know his subject. FDC indicates that there can be no blemish whatsoever and that means that no modern coins can qualify for that condition because of the method of production which causes 'bag scratches'. An item is either 'unique' or it is not.

Paper money collectors base their condition table on that of the numismatist. 'Uncirculated' is the top condition, however, and means straight from the printers. No marks or blemishes unless they were on the printing plate. Then comes 'New', 'Crisp' or the numismatic term 'EF' (Extremely Fine) which all mean hardly circulated at all but perhaps a corner crease, tiny mark or pin hole. 'Very fine' is the condition that most collectors expect to settle for. A nice pleasing note which has perhaps lost its original crispness and has been folded or creased. 'Fine' indicates that the item has obviously been in circulation but is still an attractive piece. Several folds, slightly stained, perhaps marginal tears. 'Good' is a well circulated

note beginning to look dirty and is undesirable unless of extreme rarity. 'Poor' is a bad piece. Perhaps torn in half, only semi-legible and dirty and stained.

But condition is also relative to a particular item. For example all modern bonds and banknotes can be expected to be obtained in at least 'VF' condition. There is no reason to obtain one in 'poor' condition and there is little point in hoping that such a note would ever go up in value. However, when dealing with the old private banknotes of Britain the story changes. A discerning collector will often take a piece in 'poor' condition because he has never seen it at all in fifty years of collecting. Most of these notes only turn up in 'Fine' condition at best. This is where there is no substitute for experience and knowledge. But when the note is readily available the collector should make a point of requiring his copy to be in the best possible condition, and if he does accept it in lesser condition he should be sure to see the price is adjusted accordingly.

Housing a collection is a matter of considerable importance. It is no good forming a collection of beautiful pieces if they are going to be kept in humid or damp places and left untended to the mercy of mice and insects. They will deteriorate. The first golden rule is to make sure that once every two or three years you at least flick through an album to see that no damage is becoming apparent and to let the air circulate. Albums are the best method of housing known to the collecting world at the moment. Bond collectors can get special folders for the exceptionally large items, but 90 per cent of such items can be housed in various sized specially made albums. The note collector has an even wider choice as his collection will fit nicely into the normal philatelic albums of which there is such a wide variety, as well as the specially produced banknote albums. Albums should not be stacked one on top of another as many of the items may have embossed work on them and, under such heavy pressure, these would suffer. They should be kept on bookshelves like ordinary books.

Some people worry unduly about preservation. In fact the paper on which bonds and notes are printed is very strong indeed. In normal 'home' conditions they are perfectly safe. It is only in extremes of temperatures that damage can be expected. Items of extreme rarity, and which are fragile, can now be hermetically sealed to ensure their preservation. There is always a tendency to economise on the albums in order to have more to spend on the notes. It is a false economy. A good album ensures good protection and is always well worth the money in the long run.

The special albums for banknotes contain slip-in pockets to hold the notes and show both sides, but those who use stamp albums find photo-corners or hinges adequate, the only disadvantage being that the reverse of the note cannot readily be seen.

Writing up a collection is part of the fascination of the hobby. All sorts of allied material can be used to add to the pleasure – pictures of the men who signed bonds or banknotes, pictures of the banks themselves, autographed letters of the men behind the issues and so on. A well written-up collection sets out to tell, in chronological order, the story of the subject, illustrated with examples, in a way that a non-collector can appreciate and understand what it is all about. Too many collectors, unfortunately, overlook the fact that while they may know the story behind a note, others do not: and unless they record them interesting little anecdotes may be lost in future years.

Because it is so important, most societies stage exhibitions of competitive displays, and award prizes. In the philatelic world the award of a 'gold' medal at an international exhibition invariably adds financial value to the collection if the time comes when the owner wishes to sell. The new collector can get a lot of first hand tips by going to such

societies and studying the various exhibits and ways collectors – who more often than not are individualists – have treated the presentation of their subjects.

Remember, too, that as a collection becomes 'comprehensive' it takes on an added value, far greater than the sum total of the individual notes added together. This is because the stage is reached where money alone cannot create such a collection, which has been worked on like a jig-saw puzzle to build up a complete picture. Once achieved it is naturally much more desirable than just a hotch-potch of individual items and therefore commands a higher price.

Above all, the newcomer should trust to his own judgement in which items to collect. Collect what you like, not what others tell you you should like. If you like it the chances are that others will too; if you don't like it there is a probability that others will not like it either!

The authors of this book will feel well rewarded if just a few of our readers become collectors and enter this fascinating hobby-world which has given us so much pleasure over the years.

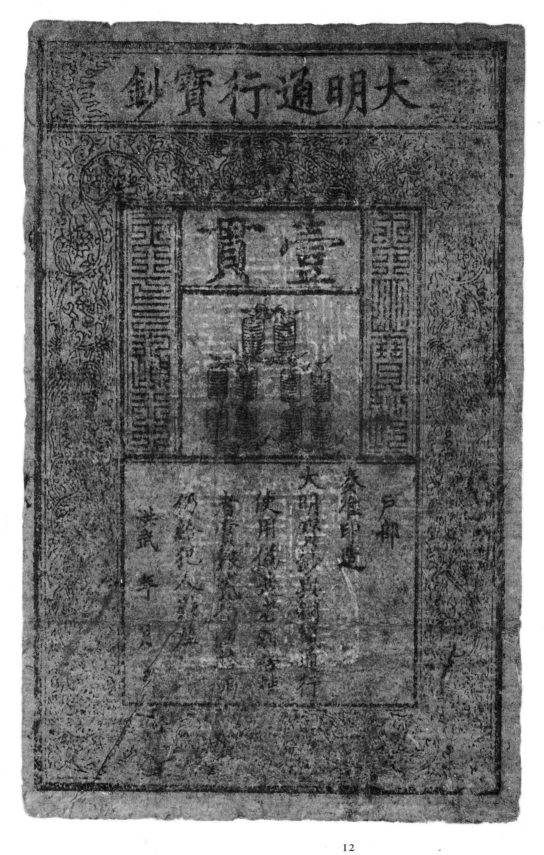

2 The Evolution of Paper Money and the Rise of Banking

Paper money owes its origins to emergencies, and the consequent hoarding of coin during those emergencies. Its rapid growth as a medium of exchange arose out of the confusion of metal money. Banks had to sort, weigh and test gold and silver from all parts of the world. The superscription of the bank on a piece of paper was soon recognised as a better certificate of valid money than the seal of the State on coin. It was not subject, as was coin, to wear and abrasion; it removed the source of profit known as 'sweating', filing and clipping, and therefore became more acceptable as a medium of payment, except for small change where metal was more convenient.

It can be said that paper money is an ideal money for the use of intelligent people – the main reason for its many failures is the inability of human nature to withstand its temptations.

The forerunner of paper money, leather, was in use in China before the birth of Christ. Emperor Wu Ti (140–87 BC) of the Western Han dynasty had white deer hides cut into one-foot squares, ornamented with floral designs and marked with high denominations. Tribute-paying warlords on their annual visit were required to purchase such a square and present it to the emperor. The custom was meticulously observed because of the emperor's propensity to behead anyone failing to follow dynastic custom.

The first recorded use of paper money is in the reign of Emperor Yung Hue of the T'ang dynasty, circa 650 AD. Such notes are described and illustrated in an early numismatic work, but the notes themselves have not survived for scholars to appraise.

Some time in the ninth century AD a form of paper money, known as 'fei-chien' (flying money) came into use, enabling horsemen to travel fast from one province to another exchanging the draft for coin on arrival at their destination. This avoided having to carry cumbersome weights of copper coins and attracting the attention of robbers.

T'ang dynasty notes were the first, as far as is known, to circulate in the manner of modern banknotes (see Glossary, page 27). Dates were hand-brushed on to the notes at the time of issue and soon wore off. But the custom of emperors to break up their reigns into periods with new titles has enabled us to place emission of many old Chinese notes to within a few years. The earliest which appears on notes is the period of Hwei Ch'ang. As the reign of the Emperor

Left: Ming Dynasty Note for 1 kwan, issued in the year 1368 AD. These notes measure 9 inches by 13 inches and were made of mulberry bark. The inscription includes 'Circulating Under the Heavens For Ever and Ever'. During the Boxer Rebellion Allied soldiers upturned statues of Buddha and found Ming notes placed under them in the manner that coins are placed under foundation stones in the West.

*Hansatsu, known affectionately among collectors'
as 'bookmark' money, spanned two centuries in
Japan with a multitude of issues. This is a silver 3
momme note of Osaka, issued in 1844.*

Wu Tsung occurred at this time, 841–847,
the issue can be dated to within six years
with certainty.

These early notes did not circulate indefinitely, each having a life of three years before
it had to be exchanged. By 1000 AD, in the
Sung dynasty, there were sixteen private
banks of issue in the Szechuan Province
alone. In an effort to control note-issues the
government set up a special bureau in 1023
and eventually took over the issue of notes
itself.

Gold and silver have always been more
highly prized than paper in Western civilisations, but in the early days of Chinese paper
money the emperors declared that it was
more desirable than cash – and to ensure
its use made it obligatory to pay proportions
of government taxes in paper money.

When the Mongols swept into China under
the banner of the famous Kublai Khan they
adopted the Chinese custom of issuing
notes. For some twenty years, while the
notes were backed by a silver system, the
issues were successful. Then they caused the
world's first great paper money inflation.
Essentially conquerors, their commitments
to hold territory by the sword got out of
hand and they resorted to the printing press
to pay their soldiers. By 1358 AD their paper
money was worthless and their power had
waned in China.

The first descriptions of paper money given
to the West come from this time when such
people as Marco Polo wrote: 'They are so
light that ten bezants' worth does not weigh
one golden bezant... and with this paper
money the merchants can buy what they like
anywhere over the Empire whilst it is also
vastly lighter to carry about on their
journeys'.

Early in the Ming dynasty paper money was
declared the only legal tender and for a time
it became an offence to transact business in
gold or silver. Ming notes, circa 1368 AD,
are the earliest paper money generally available to collectors. They survived because

they are made of strong mulberry bark paper and because many were put under statues of Buddha in the manner that Western civilisations put coins under foundation stones. During the Boxer Rebellion soldiers looting in Peking upturned statues and they were found. They are large notes, measuring 13 inches by 9, and written on them is the statement that they 'Circulate Under the Heavens Forever and Ever'. The notes offer high reward for the detection of counterfeiting, which indicates that at that time forgery of note-issues was a serious problem for the Chinese government.

Inflation on a scale equal to that of the great German hyper-inflation of the 1920s occurred in the Ming dynasty and by 1436 the government stopped issuing paper money. For two hundred years no official paper money was to circulate in China. Then, in 1651, an issue known as Kuan Chao was made. But memories of inflation must have still been strong as the issue was not accepted and a few years later was withdrawn altogether.

Not until the emergency caused by the T'ai Ping Rebellion of 1854–1859 did paper money appear again in China.

Japan was not so far behind China with the issue of notes and many of the early ones are known as 'Hansatsu'. They were actually used as bookmarks when they first came to the attention of the West, because of their size and shape. The first appeared during the reign of the Emperor Daigo (1334) but notes did not circulate widely until the time of Tokugawa (1542–1616). The proud Japanese Daimios had a code of chivalry and honour that the West had left behind at Agincourt. It followed that this warrior class soon found itself in debt to the rising merchant class and, to overcome this, the Shoguns issued promissory notes in the form of hansatsu. They first appeared in the eighteenth century.

The introduction of paper money in the West came at a much later date than in China. A form of paper money is said to have been issued in 1250 by James I of Catalonia and Arragon although none has survived. It is known that the founded banks such as loan-offices and insurance banks as well as maritime consulates. In 1401 the Exchange Bank in Barcelona re-established monetary documents though they cannot be considered as paper money in the normal sense. Some Spanish authorities maintain that issues of emergency paper money were made in 1483 (Siege of Alhambra) and 1490 (Siege of Granada) but no supporting evidence has yet come to light. Indeed, the earliest Spanish notes would appear to the Royal Securities of Charles III, issued in 1799, of which the Valencia Museum possesses 1000 and 100 *real* notes.

Generally accepted as the first paper money of Europe, as distinct from banknotes, are the Leyden emergency issues. Money was struck on coin presses using planchets made from compressed book pages, usually Bibles and Books of Hours. Responsible for their issue was the famous Burgermaster Pieter Andriaanszoon van der Werf who in 1574 introduced the new currency, telling his people: 'You may eat me first. I will not surrender to the Spanish'. The siege took place during the Netherlands' eighty-year war with Spain and Leyden suffered terrible privation and starvation. A boy, Cornelius Jospensz, was the first to notice the Spanish raising the siege, but the city elders did not really believe him and offered him six guilders to go and find out. The Spanish had gone, but had left a full pot of stew which took the total attention of the boy. Impatient for news, the city elders finally went out themselves to find the boy with an empty stew pot in one hand, waving happily with the other. A bronze statue marks the spot and the pot is the most prized possession of the city's Lakenhal Museum. *Hutspot* – the stew – is eaten to this day in the Netherlands on 3 October to mark the anniversary of the raising of the siege.

The first banknotes to be issued in the West were those of the Swedish Stockholm Bank, and appeared on 16 July 1661.

Founded by Johan Palmstruch in 1660, the Stockholm Bank found itself in trouble in its first year on account of the Swedish currency depreciation. A general run on the bank looked as if it would bring disaster and Palmstruch played for time until a sufficient quantity of new coins could be struck by creating Kreditvsedlar (notes of credit).

It is interesting to note that in 1652 Palmstruch had in fact recommended that payment of large amounts should be made by Banckbrieflein (small bank letters).

Professor E.F.Heckscher, the Swedish economist and historian, wrote that this invention of banknotes constituted Palmstruch's claim to a place in the history of money and banking. The promissory notes (see Glossary, page 27) created later in the same century by English and Scottish banks were of the same character and influenced future development infinitely more, but Palmstruch was responsible for their 'forerunners'.

Norway also had a very early issue of paper money in 1695. Jorgen Thor Mohlen built up an empire of businesses producing ropes, soap, oil, woollen goods, gunpowder and

Sweden holds the honour of issuing (in 1661) the first true banknotes in Europe. Most of the surviving specimens are dated 1666 and bear eight signatures, including Johan Palmstruch whose idea they were.

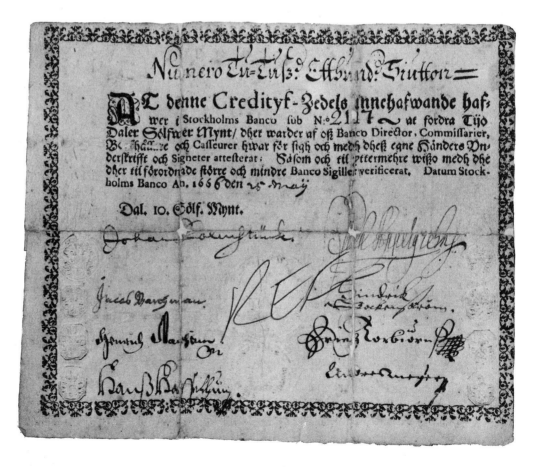

various other things. He became the richest man in Norway, and virtually economic adviser to the government. His success depended on his ships which did heavy trade all over the world. Wars among the European powers caused him to lose many vessels and when his creditors began to grow alarmed Mohlen asked the king for permission to issue paper money, the idea being that it would circulate until his trading ships returned from overseas. Unfortunately, the people did not trust this paper money and presented it for redemption as soon as they received it. Mohlen went bankrupt and died insolvent in 1709.

On the other side of the Atlantic, severe restrictions and outright prohibition of coin to the American colonies caused a great scarcity and many items were introduced to replace it. Among them was wampum (beads from the inner whorls of the *pirula carica* or canaliculata periwinkle shells). In 1640 Massachusetts set a value of 4d for the white and 2d for the blue. By 1641 wampum was made lawful money for any sum under £10.

In the South, tobacco was declared legal tender and the first law of the General Assembly of Virginia, 31 July 1619, was drafted for the purpose of fixing its price. Tobacco was kept in public warehouses and receipts were issued to depositers. These warehouse receipts quickly came to be used as actual money. Virginian Law recognised this in 1641 and to protect the scarce coin enacted that no debts contracted to be paid in coin could be sued in a court of law (Noble Foster Hoggson, *Epochs in American Banking*).

Virginia issued notes redeemable in tobacco in 1705 and by 1727 these notes were made legal tender. Massachussetts, however, issued the first normal type of paper money in 1690 to meet the pay of soldiers returning from the disastrous expedition against the French in Canada. The government had been totally unprepared for their early

return, and seems to have presumed not only upon victory, but upon the capture of treasure! As the soldiers were on the point of mutiny notes were hurriedly issued in denominations of 2s. to £10 and were declared valid for paying taxes.

Playing cards were to become the first paper money of Canada. The first issues were made by Jacques de Meulles, Intendant in 1685. His letters explaining the issue to the King, Louis XIV of France, have survived. One, addressed to 'My Lord' and dated 'Quebec September 24, 1685', states: 'I have found myself this year in great straits with regard to the subsistence of the soldiers. You did not provide for funds, My Lord, until January last. I have, notwithstanding, kept them in provisions until September, which makes eight full months. I have drawn from my own funds and from those of my friends, all I have been able to get, but at last finding them without means to render me further assistance, and not knowing to what Saint to pay my vows, money being extremely scarce, having distributed considerable sums on every side for the pay of soldiers, it occurred to me to issue, instead of money, notes on cards, which I have had cut in quarters. I send you My Lord, three kinds, one is for four francs, another for 40 sols and the third for 15 sols... no person has refused them'.

Another letter to the French King, this time the young Louis XV, dated 1729 records: My Lord, M. Hocquart had the honour to inform you in Paris that he had made a purchase of about 2,000 sets of cards, blank on both sides, to provide for the making of card money ordered by His Majesty. Two-thirds of them have been soaked in water and entirely ruined in the wreck of the King's ship. We shall be obliged to use ordinary cards... We beg you My Lord to have sent by next year's ship, 2,000 sets of 52 cards each in order that we may be in a position to make new money'.

The hyper-inflation of Germany in the 1920s caused the issue of 20, 50 and 100 billion mark notes by the Reichsbank. At the height of the inflation a 100 billion mark note was worth about £7. Workers were paid twice daily and given time to go shopping before the value was eroded by inflation.

In Russia plans were drawn up as early as the reign of Peter the Great (1689–1725) for the issue of paper money, but foreign loans and additional revenue through the expansion of imports and exports overcame the problem and made the issue unnecessary.

Usually Catherine the Great (1762–1796) is credited with the first Russian paper money in 1769. It is possible, however, that paper money was first printed in 1762 during the reign of Peter III. Potemkin, as Minister of War, is said to have left behind a personal library containing volumes bound in pigskin and made up of 1000-rouble notes. It was not until 1886 that 1000-rouble notes became known to scholars, and the reported volumes of Potemkin are not available for examination.

Early banknotes of Poland came about through the War of Independence of 1794. They turn up in remarkably good condition because they did not circulate for long – war overtook and ruthlessly crushed the leaders of the insurrection.

The notes remain a testimony to a great man of freedom – Tadeusz Kosciuszko – a man whose place in history had already been assured when he fought at the side of George Washington in the American War of Independence.

The death without heir of King Jan Sobieski gave rise to foreign intervention and Kosciuszko led the Polish insurrection, supported by both rich and poor – an unusual circumstance for any revolution. He issued the famous paper money Independence notes, but his rebellion was not successful. The notes are headed: 'Resolution of the Highest Council of the Nation'.

Most of the early notes of the world came about through war. In Africa the early pioneers were quick to resort to paper money. With coin in short supply in the Cape, six-dollar notes were printed in 1782, a year after the outbreak of war between England and the Netherlands.

In the Boer War both Kruger and Colonel

Baden-Powell issued special notes. The last of the Kruger notes were issued 'In the Field'; Baden-Powell designed notes himself during the siege of Mafeking.

Inflation saw immense amounts of paper money being issued, in subsequent periods. For instance, Edward Atterton, in his treatise on the hyperinflation of Germany in the 1920s informs us that at its height, the number of marks to the pound equalled the number of yards to the sun.

The paper money of modern times is every bit as interesting as the issues of olden days. The size of paper money gets smaller, reflecting the high cost of paper – once a £1 note was the size of the old white fiver; now it is smaller than the wartime 10 shilling note. Currency reforms are marked with special issues of notes and backed by national campaigns to promote the change, such as in Australia when the currency was changed to the decimal system.

The new collector will find a great deal of interest in forming a collection of modern notes of the world which often depict the new rulers of emergent nations who have found paper money a good medium for propaganda. Some of the newly formed territories do not last long and consequently their paper money issues are soon scarce. For example, Moise Tshombe declared Katanga an independent republic in 1960 and immediately issued paper money with his portrait, having deposed the luckless Patrice Lumumba. In his turn Tshombe was denounced by Colonel Mobutu whose portrait appeared on notes after he had sentenced Tshombe to death, one of the charges being the illegal issue of paper money. Although Tshombe escaped to Spain he was subsequently hi-jacked and died in mysterious circumstances at the

The highest denomination of 'invasion money', 5000 French francs. Counterfeitors worked so quickly that their notes were on the market before the issue date – and consequently the 5000 francs was withdrawn altogether. On the reverse is the tricolour, to which General de Gaulle took exception because 'only a Frenchman has the right to use the tricolour'. In deference to him the tricolour was omitted from subsequent issues of the Allied Military currency. Collectors use the name 'invasion money' because the lower denominations were carried over the beaches on D-Day on the orders of General Eisenhower, after failing to reach agreement with the French Committee of National Liberation.

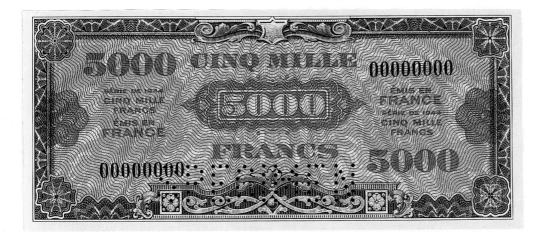

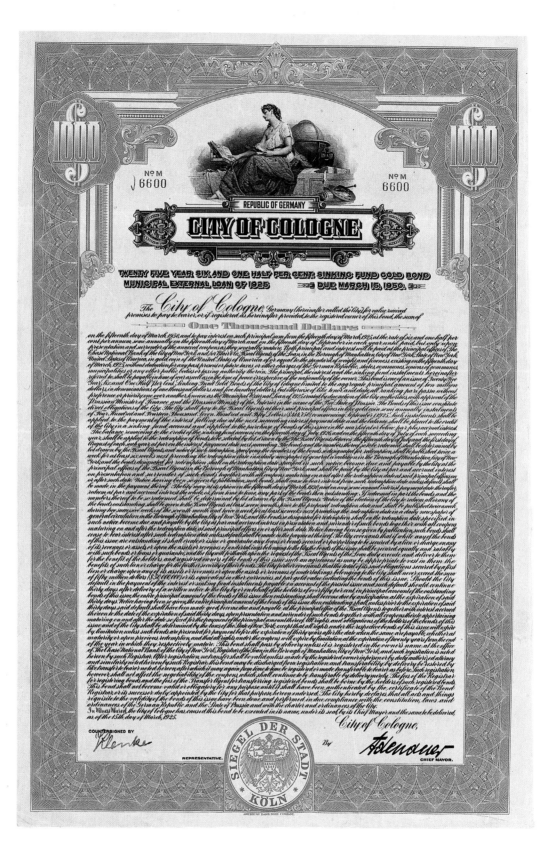

REPUBLIC OF GERMANY

CITY OF COLOGNE

TWENTY FIVE YEAR SIX AND ONE HALF PER CENT SINKING FUND GOLD BOND
MUNICIPAL EXTERNAL LOAN OF 1925 — DUE MARCH 15, 1950.

No M 6600

No M 6600

$1000

The *City of Cologne*, Germany (hereinafter called the City) for value received promises to pay to bearer, or if registered as hereinafter provided, to the registered owner of this bond, the sum of

One Thousand Dollars

COUNTERSIGNED BY

Klenke

REPRESENTATIVE.

City of Cologne,

By Adenauer

CHIEF MAYOR.

SIEGEL DER STADT ★ KÖLN ★

hands of Mobutu's agents. Biafra is another example of a short-lived territory with paper money that was to become valueless, except to collectors, within a short space of time. Some of the new leaders ensure that flattering portraits of themselves are used on notes, among them Idi Amin.

The ever-changing political situations in the world often cause issues of new paper money which, formed into a collection, can well illustrate the progress of modern times.

The rise of banking

Early banking in the West tended to be limited because of usury laws. It was not until Henry VIII legalised the taking of interest that banking really started to expand. For although modern civilisation is based on making loans and paying interest it was not always so. For a thousand years the Christian Church was totally opposed to the taking of interest which was outlawed by canon and civil law until the sixteenth century. Aristotle and Cicero were among the great thinkers of antiquity who advised against interest taking. Statutes of Alfred, William the Conqueror, Henry II, Henry III, Edward I, Edward III and Henry VII prohibited the lending of money upon interest with penalties ranging from forfeiture of chattels, lands and Christian burial, to perpetual banishment.

Early banks were simply banks of deposit and the bankers made their living by charging a fee for handling the affairs of their depositors. Such banks were introduced as adjuncts to public granary systems, by the ancient Egyptians and the early Greeks.

The practice of bankers to use deposited valuables as the backing for issues of paper money was not permitted for many years. An edict of the Venetian Senate in 1361 forbade bankers to engage in mercantile pursuits and, because they started using 'dummies', they were, a few years later, forbidden

the creation of credit against certain commodities. In 1526 the use of cheques, by which one banker paid off his deposits by a draft on another bank, was also forbidden (F. F. Dunbar, *The Bank of Venice*, 1892). Clearly these early bankers were not faced with the risk of bank robbery that exists today, for laws also required current funds to be on view and for all payments to be made over the counter *(sopra il banco)*. Bankers managed to find ways round the laws and in 1584 the failure of the House of Pisani and Tiepolo for 500,000 ducats brought private banking to an end in Venice. The State created its own bank, the Banco della Piazza del Rialto, which did not attempt to make profit from the use of its credit, but only from fees for transactions.

It was the Italians who invented the modern bill of exchange (see Glossary, page 27). Forms of such bills of exchange were used by the Assyrians from the ninth to the seventh centuries BC and were widely used by the *publicani,* the bankers of the Roman world, but in the sense of modern usage it was the Florentine and Genoese merchants who introduced the bill of exchange. This had a marked effect on commerce as it was no longer necessary to bring large quantities of actual wares to the great city fairs. Sales could be made by samples as the bills could

Left: With the introduction of the currency reform of 1923, Germany returned to economic sanity after the post-war years of galloping inflation. As from 1924, with international confidence restored, Germany became the world's largest borrower, mainly helped by the United States whose position as lender was pre-eminent. This $1000 bond of the City of Cologne Municipal External Loan, signed by K. Adenauer as Mayor of the town, was issued in New York on 15 March 1925. Ironically, the test of the loan agreement states that 'the principal, the interest and the sinking fund instalments shall be payable in time of war as well as in the time of peace'. Together with over a hundred other dollar issues, this loan went into default during the 1930s following the Great Crash. Most of this foreign debt was eventually settled by the London Debt Agreement, a treaty signed by the Federal Republic of Germany and several other countries in 1953.

be payable to order, drawn in the money of another country where it was due, payable in a specified place, or where a cargo was discharged on a specific date or twenty days after sight.

Some of the great centres of banking should be mentioned. Florence, which gave its name to the gold florin first coined there in 1252, became a major banking centre during the early republic and was dominated by the Medici family, known as bankers in 1434. Parchment promissory notes were issued during the rule of the Grand Duke Cosimo III de' Medici (1670–1723).

Hamburg took on some importance with the creation of the Bank of Hamburg which maintained the principles of early banking, refusing to overissue credit on deposits. No loans were made beyond the amount of coin deposited and only Hamburg citizens could open accounts. Napoleon expressed surprise when his troops took over the Bank on 5 November 1813 and found 7,506,956 marks in silver held against liabilities of only 7,489,343. In 1816 the French were obliged to return the treasure and the bank was able to resume business with unimpaired credit.

Amsterdam was another great centre of banking and in 1609 the Bank of Amsterdam was founded on the principle that deposits were the property of the depositor and not for the use of the bank for making profit. Although the bank's accounts were kept secret the city's committee was required to take an annual oath that the deposits were all there. In fact, the committee made large loans, particularly to the East India Company, which resulted in insolvency, the bank ceasing to exist in 1819. Antwerp took over as the great merchant centre and banking centre of Europe in the sixteenth century. Bruges had developed as the main centre but when the Zwin silted up preventing ships from using Bruges, there was a general migration of merchants and bankers to Antwerp. Also, Antwerp gave absolute freedom to merchants and bankers. There were no restrictions on trade in money, precious metals or bills. It is said that at its height more than five hundred vessels sailed in or out of Antwerp per day and that the English employed more than 20,000 people in the city.

Formation of joint stock companies

When Henry VIII made interest-taking legal, there was a great surge of speculative banking. Merchants would borrow in one market and lend in another where there was a more favourable rate. This saw the introduction of more paper money and the beginnings of the joint stock companies.

These companies developed from merchant guilds. A guild, an Anglo-Saxon word meaning a contribution to a common fund, was formed by a group of merchants agreeing to travel together for common protection. From the guilds came the regulated companies which were associations of merchants required by European governments to be formed so that permanent trade could be established. In point of fact they enabled the government to tax and regulate them with greater ease. Two such companies were the English Muscovy Company (1556) trading with Russia and the East India Company (1599).

The demands of greater permanence and stronger authority saw the gradual transformation to joint stock enterprises and by 1700 there were 140 joint stock companies in England and Scotland.

The major joint stock companies, which issued their own paper money, were the East India, the African, Hudson's Bay and New River Companies, and the Bank of England. The first two voyages of the English East India company made 95 per cent profit, though it took over nine years to close the accounts (J. W. Jeudwine, *Studies in Empire and Trade,* London 1923).

Pay warrant hand-signed (at top left) by Henry VIII, dated 1514. It reads:
'We wool and commade you that of our money being in your keeping you do
paye and deliver unto our servant Lancaster one of our Heralds the somm of
seven pounds thirteen shillings and four pence farthinge for such cost and
charge as he hath susteigned by our commandment to and from us and our citie
of Tournay and these letters shall be your sufficient warrant and discharge in
this behalf given under our signet at our manor at Eltham the 12th day of July
the sixthyere of our reign. To our trusty and well beloved knight for our body
Sir Robert Dymmok Treasurer of our citie of Tournay.' (Sir Robert Dymmok
was king's champion at the coronations of Richard III, Henry VII and
Henry VIII.)

23

Banking in England

Goldsmiths were the fathers of the modern paper money system. Mr Lawson in his *History of Banking* tells us that the first private bankers in England were Jews who were robbed and persecuted under a successsion of sovereigns until their oppression culminated in the reign of Edward I who seized the possessions of 15,000 Jews and then banished them.

The vacuum was filled by the Lombards, or Longobards, from Italy, who gave their name to Lombard Street. The earliest record we have of goldsmith bankers comes from the *Little London Directory* published in 1677 which records that in that year there were thirty-seven goldsmiths who kept running-cashes (ie. acted as bankers) in Lombard Street.

Charles I, piqued when the City of London refused him a loan, seized the money which had been deposited in the Royal Mint in the Tower of London by the goldsmith bankers, thereby ruining many of them. It was not surprising therefore that the Goldsmiths' Company subscribed cash and men to help Cromwell in the Civil War.

Goldsmith bankers were able to increase during the Commonwealth and the practice became general for them to issue notes. These were receipts or cash-notes payable on demand against the plate or metal coin deposited with them. As they represented actual value the notes were passed from hand to hand and became known as goldsmith notes. Later, during the early days of the Restoration, the goldsmiths were in the habit of depositing their surplus cash with the Exchequer, and for this they received interest from the King.

Their downfall came when Charles II let it be known that he would make any man Lord Treasurer of England if he found a way for the King to obtain £1,500,000. Sir Thomas Clifford suggested he simply closed the Exchequer where such a sum was deposited by goldsmiths. The King did just that, and Clifford thus became Lord High Treasurer for 'stealing' from the goldsmiths.

The first paper money to enjoy legal tender status in England was the Exchequer Order of Charles II. In 1696 it was replaced with the Exchequer Bill. The order differed from the bill in that it was payable on demand in cash, whereas an elaborate system was set up to convert bills, and funds for this were provided by making bills a charge upon the proceeds of certain state revenues. Technically, therefore, while the bill was good money it was in fact a form of investment, a short-term government loan. It was the Bank of England that put paid to the Exchequer Bill, for in 1707 it was entrusted with the guarantee and redemption of these bills. Naturally there was more profit to the Bank in promoting their own notes so the bills gradually passed out of use.

It comes as a surprise to many people to learn that the banknotes of this time, including those of the Bank of England, were private paper accepted only by custom and devoid of any legal tender status. It was not until the Act of 3–4 William IV in 1833 that a limited legal tender status was accorded by Parliament to the Bank of England notes. Today the Bank of England is the pivot of the British economy, yet its foundation was almost hidden in a Bill which made it possible. Lord Macaulay wrote of it: 'It was... not easy to guess that a Bill which purported only to impose a new duty on tonnage for the benefit of such persons as should advance money towards carrying on the war, was really a Bill creating the greatest commercial institution that the world has ever seen'.

The Bank of England had a hard time in its formative years. Within two years of its foundation it was forced to suspend payments, a situation which lasted from July 1695 to 1697 and resulted in depreciation of notes which fell to a discount of 17 per cent. This was not really surprising considering that the accounts submitted to the House of Commons on 4 December 1696 showed notes outstanding to be £764,196 supported by cash of only £35,664.

In 1707 the Old Pretender threatened to invade England and caused a run on the Bank of England. Two goldsmith bankers, Sir R. Hoare and Sir Francis Child, used the opportunity to join forces and try to break the Bank of England by presenting large amounts of bank bills for payment. The Bank, however, was able to weather the storm.

Another difficult time came with the collapse of the South Sea Bubble in 1720 when a run occurred on the Bank. It was met by making payments in light sixpences and shillings and by engaging men to fill up the line, draw money and redeposit it at another window. It also happened that the feast of Michaelmas came at that time which allowed the bank to close while the panic subsided. The Bank of England had to resort to the same tactics during the initial success of the Pretender in 1707.

During the next thirty years the Bank of England operated with growing success and a number of institutions opened up banking businesses till at one time nearly 400 note-issuing banks were operating. But the wars

Bank of England £1000 note. The 'white' notes of the Bank of England were issued from 1725 to 1956 and the last £1000 note was issued in 1943. It was this series of notes which was heavily forged by the Axis powers. The famous spy Cicero received his payment in forged white fivers.

Bank Stock.

Dividends due

April 5th
Oct'. 10th
and are usually paid the day after.

Transfer Days

Tuesday.
Thursday.
Friday.
Holidays excepted.

Received this 5th Day of Dec'. 1834

of *Abraham Tozer Esq*

the Sum of *Forty nine pounds 10/0*

Sterling, being the Consideration for *Twenty two pounds three shillings* Interest or Share in the Capital Stock and Funds of the Governor and Company of the **BANK of ENGLAND**, by *me* this Day transferred to the said *Abraham Tozer Esq*

Witness *my* Hand the Day of the Date above-written.

Witness

The Proprietors to protect themselves from F·R·A·U·D, are recommended to ACCEPT by themselves or their Attorneys, all TRANSFERS made to them.

£.	s.	d.
49.	10.	0

Such 'inscribed' stock receipts as this one, dated 5 December 1834, were issued by the Bank of England to brokers acting on behalf of clients purchasing or selling Bank of England stock but unable to sign in person the 'inscribed book' at the Bank of England. This was performed by the brokers with power of attorney. Note at the top right the price of the Bank's stock: 223½.

---

with France and the struggle in the American colonies caused a collapse of credit in 1797. One third of all English banks had to suspend payment, including the Bank of England. The suspension continued through the Napoleonic Wars and it was not until 1816 that there was a partial resumption of specie payments, which then had to be postponed until 1821 when the Bank began redeeming its own issue at a discount.

The first real attack on unsound paper money issues did not come until 1844 when Sir Robert Peel's Bank Act was passed with his avowed intention to make the Bank of England notes 'as good as gold'. Bank of England notes were made to represent 'warehouse receipts' for the actual metallic money. To achieve this the note issue department was separated from the banking department so that gold held against note issue would be clearly identified, and not confounded with reserves held against deposits. The Act allowed a maximum of £14 million uncovered notes – supported by government bonds and not gold. This was based on the minimum amount of notes which could always be expected to remain in circulation – during 1839 at the height of the run on the Bank circulation had not fallen below £14,732,000. While country banks were still allowed to issue it was anticipated that many would become insolvent and others would go out of business as their charter expired. The private, provincial and joint-stock companies were gradually absorbed by larger companies and their powers curtailed by the government's refusal to renew note-issuing licenses. By 1921 private banknotes had ceased in England (Fox, Fowler Ltd. made the last issue in that year). However, it was not until 1961 that issues in the Isle of Man were taken over by the Isle of Man government. Until then Barclays, Lloyds, Westminster and Martins were popular notes in the island. Scotland, which boasts the most colourful of all British paper money, still has three banks issuing notes, the Bank of Scotland, the Royal Bank and the Clydesdale Bank.

More and more interest is being shown in the early bank issues which so aptly reflect the development of nations, and recall the individuals of the past whose tenacity and drive led to the giant banking institutions.

A short glossary of the types of paper money in use

PROMISSORY NOTE
An unconditional promise in writing made by one person to another signed by the maker, engaging to pay, on demand or at a fixed time, a sum of money to the order of a specified person or to bearer.

BANKNOTE
A promissory note issued by a bank and payable to bearer on demand; but unlike promissory notes they may be re-issued after payment.

BILL OF EXCHANGE
An unconditional order in writing, addressed by one person to another, signed by the person giving it requiring the person to whom it is addressed to pay on demand or at a fixed time.

SIGHT BILL
A bill of exchange payable 'at sight'. Equivalent to a bill payable on demand. When 'after sight' (eg. 20 days after sight) the date is calculated from the date of acceptance.

CHEQUE
A bill of exchange drawn on a banker, payble on demand. A cheque differs from a bill in several ways, the most important being that it does not require acceptance.
The word is derived from the French *échecs*, chess. The chequers placed at the doors of public houses indicated that chess was played there. Similar tables were employed in reckoning money, and hence came the expression 'to check an account'. The government office where the public accounts were kept was called the 'Exchequer'.

3

The Art of Banknotes

One of the most specialized sections of the printing industry is security printing. With the aim to be always one step ahead of any forger the resulting product shows great ingenuity and beauty. In order to appreciate these aspects to their full extent we must examine both the methods of production, and the people behind paper money issues. Direct Printing (DP), Intaglio or Deep Print is by far the most important and most skilled form of engraving. DP is carried out using a graver or burin. An engraver will often make his own graver, which is basically a wedge-shaped steel instrument with a wooden handle. Today the graver is used to cut a line in soft steel, although up to the early nineteenth century copper was used. A skilled engraver can cut a line and tell its depth to within a few microns. Engraving a line is often a two-cut process because as the graver comes out of the steel it forms a 'tail off', resulting in a triangular cut. In order to even up the cut it is necessary to turn the plate round and cut in the opposite direction. This way a basically dumb-bell-shaped hole is produced. Because of the great sensitivity of cut available by this method and with the use of semi-translucent ink DP can produce a form of perspective available to no other method. DP is carried out by covering the engraved plate with a glutinous ink which fills the recesses cut by engraving. The surface of the plate is then wiped clean. The paper is laid

The tools used for engraving a steel plate. The graver is on the far right-hand side and a plate of the Ionian Bank £2 note, 184–. Their Zante branch, engraved by Perkins Bacon and Petch, is in the background.

Left above: Belgian Banque Nationale 10,000 Franc note – 2000 Belgas, 7 December 1929; an elaborate vignette showing four-in-hands to left and right, a lion in the centre and various allegorical figures. Engraved by G. Minguet.

Left below: Reverse of the above note but engraved by M. Poortman.

on the plate either wet or dry and using high pressure the paper is forced into the recesses where it picks up the ink. On drying a lovely crisp raised relief print is formed.

Lithographic, litho or flat printing is one of the most common commercial methods of printing. Litho is basically printing off a raised surface and is, therefore, the opposite of DP. The plate used in litho is usually produced by minutely etching or very lightly washing away the parts of the plate that are not wanted. Imagine a lino cut produced by most children at school. A thin layer of ink is put across the top of the plate and this is then printed directly, or transferred by roller, to paper.

Letterpress or high print is the third basic type of printing used in the production of banknotes and is very similar to litho except that it is always a direct printing onto paper. Letterpress is most commonly used for putting serial numbers, dates, and where possible, signatures on notes. When an order

for banknotes comes into a security printer it goes to the Preliminaries or 'Prelims' Department. In Prelims the first step in the process is to 'rough out' a design or produce what the Americans call a 'model'. This 'rough out' is often a composite picture probably incorporating particular flora, fauna or a building that has special significance to the country of origin. As far as possible this 'rough out' will be done from pictures but in some cases it may be necessary for the artist to visit the country concerned. By the time the alterations have been made to a design and it has been finally approved by the client, a period of some four months may have elapsed although normally this period is much shorter. From the approved rough a watercolour will be produced in such detail that even single hair detail brushes are used. The reason for this minute detail is because the engraver will work from this painting; and therefore it must be actual size. The engravers will transfer the facets

Banque Centrale du Mali 5000 Franc note, undated but issued between 1971 and 1973. It is interesting to compare the vibrant colouring of this contemporary note with the pastel printing of the Belgian 10,000 franc note on page 28.

of pencil and brushwork with its depth, lightness, and detail to a medium featuring all these textures but achieving it with only a gradation in depth of line.

A trainee engraver will spend about seven years under basic training and during this time it is doubtful whether any commercial work will be undertaken. After this initial period of training he will be allowed to do some letter engraving and perhaps some minor detail work. After about fifteen years' training the engraver should be proficient enough to do vignette work, but portrait engraving cannot be tackled before much under twenty to twenty-five years' training. Alan Dow of Bradbury Wilkinson & Co. was quite exceptional when he started to engrave portraits several years before the end of this normal period. He produced the Queen's and the Duke of Wellington's portrait on our current five-pound note, and also executed the Queen's portrait on the twenty-pound note; this took him six months to do.

Some peculiar traits develop in engravers during the course of their work. Although they work with both eyes open, one eye will develop much more than the other, which becomes lazy. If they need to wear glasses in later life the master eye may well only have plain glass in front of it. Whether the continued use of binocular microscopes reduces this occurrence only time will tell. Another curious fact is that an engraver can read a paper held up to a mirror more quickly than the normal way, although this is really not too surprising when one considers that he spends most of his life working back-to-front.

Types of engraving

In the production of a master plate various engravers are responsible for different parts of the note. In training engravers tend towards a speciality in a particular area. The first of these areas is portrait engraving, which is perhaps the most difficult and often the most important because people prominent in public life are invariably depicted. The portrait engraver, as previously explained, takes the longest to train. Secondly, there is vignette engraving which depicts trees, mountains, people in situations and buildings etc. Thirdly, there is letter engraving, and this is the name of the bank, text and various other details. In the nineteenth century there was another type of engraving called 'stump' engraving, and this was used to produce minute lettering of either the name of the bank or the denomination of the note up to a thousand times in the centre of the note.

There are two other types of engraving, both of which are done on a machine. The first of these types is achieved by use of a machine called the geometrical lathe. The geometrical lathe was invented by an American called Asa Spencer who was inspired by the line work found on French clocks and watches. Asa Spencer's machine in fact looked nothing like a lathe but more like a huge gear box on legs. The principle of the machine is that by use of various horizontally based discs and gear wheels all moving together and by using different settings an

Czechoslovakian Ministry of Finance 500 Korun note, 15 April 1919. This note was designed by the famous Czechoslovakian artist Alfons Mucha in the Art Deco style.

31

Banque du Canada $25 note, 6 May 1935. Bearing portrait vignettes of King George V and Queen Mary and printed by the Canadian Bank Note Company, this is the rarer French text variety. A reverse vignette shows Windsor Castle.

Icelandic Islands Banki 10 Kronur note, 1920. Printed by Giesecke & Devrient of Germany.

almost infinite number of geometrical designs can be produced. A very simple comparison of this type of machine can be found in a child's game which uses toothed circular plastic discs which can be rotated within discs to produce simple spiralled geometric patterns. In the geometric lathe a diamond-tipped point is lowered onto a plate held on top of the moving gear box and this point cuts the design into the plate. By noting the settings on the discs and gearwheels the printer can reproduce at will literally millions of designs. By the use of the transfer press, a machine which will be explained in a moment, this process can be taken a step further to produce white-line work in which the lines appear white on a black background.

Relief or medal engraving is the second type of mechanical engraving. In this process a model – such as the head on a coin – is fixed in place on the machine. An arm with a stylus or master pin runs up and down over the area on which the coin is placed. This point is connected by pivots to a diamond tip which itself runs up and down over a waxed plate. The stylus creates a straight line on the plate until it touches the coin. When this happens the vertical undulations of the coin produce a horizontal deviation of the diamond tip. When the machine has finished its run the waxed plate is taken off and etched. If all the different engravings were to be done on one plate it would take years to produce a finished master plate instead of a few months as is the case. This is achieved by using a method called transference or transferring. The transfer press was invented by Jacob Perkins as a natural progression to the work he had been doing on steel engraving. Up to the early nineteenth century engraving was carried out on copper, a fast wearing metal only capable of producing about 5000 prints per plate, but Perkins found that by using soft steel and then tempering it he could increase production to about 30,000 prints per plate. Having done this he produced the transfer press. Each engraver responsible for his piece of work, letter, vignette etc. does so within a specified area of a plate. Each piece of work is then taken in turn and placed on the transfer press. The press is one of the few pieces of machinery that security printers have not been able to make automatic with any success. It looks like a metal bench with a ten-foot-high ship's wheel attached to one side. By gently easing a soft steel roller back and forth across each plate a raised relief is formed. Each piece of engraving is put on until the roller has a

Portuguese Banco de Portugal 100 MilReis note, 10 March 1909. A large vignette showing the return of Cabral, having claimed Brazil for Portugal in 1500.

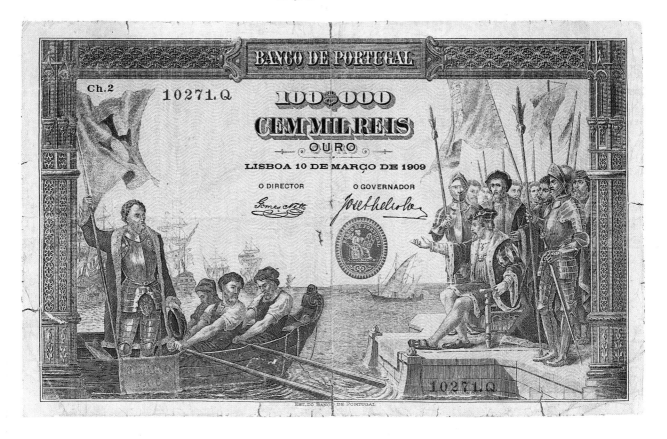

33

The Sunderland Bank £5 note, 18– (printer's proof). This English bank started in 1816 and was taken over in 1836. Engraved by W.H. Lizars, note the 'stump engraving' in the centre, where the denomination appears nearly five hundred times.

Reverse of Banco de España 1000 pesetas, 1 May 1895. Note the fine 'Medallion engraved' head left of centre.

composite picture on it. If the roller is then chemically or heat hardened the process can be reversed so that a plate for intaglio printing can be made up. Transference can be simply summed up as a female – male – female process. The completed plate with an absolutely uniform impression on it is then hardened, perhaps chromed to increase life and curved to fit on the press, a process which itself can take up to three days to complete.

Printing banknotes

The paper used by security printers is of very high quality, because it must be able to withstand a fair amount of circulation, and it is produced almost entirely from pure linen scraps. Plastic has been tried as an alternative but as yet the same quality of print cannot be attained and quite frankly it lasts too long! During paper manufacture several security features may be included in the paper. The watermark is added by binding wire on a wire net held in a wooden frame. When the pulp is laid the paper is thinned or thickened by the binding so that on drying the watermark appears as a lighter patch in the paper. In America security threads are favoured. These threads are usually coloured or multicoloured and are introduced into the paper either in the pulp or just as the pulp is poured into the frame. Some threads are actually printed with the name of the bank and others are only visible under ultra-violet light. Banknote paper may also have invisible fluorescence which is a chemical in the paper which will fluoresce under ultra-violet light. Normally the fluorescence will be the denomination spotted on various parts of the note.

Ink is produced by the printers using their own recipes. The ink used in Intaglio print-

ing is thick and glutinous and although it produces a much crisper type of print it has the disadvantage of taking a long time to dry. Intaglio ink must have that special quality to print both the thick and thin lines of a plate to the utmost definition. Because of the difference in line the ink must be able to give them their proper emphasis. One type of ink that most of us are familiar with is that used on the old Bank of England notes. The ink has that very subtle velvety black look obtained by boiling charcoal produced from German grape vines in linseed oil. The name of this ink is Frankfort Black.

Hong Kong and Shanghai Banking Corporation
$10 note, 1 July 1913. A beautifully engraved and
printed note by Waterlow & Sons Ltd.

Spanish Banco de Espana 1000 Pesetas note, 1 May 1895. Note the three watermarks and security threads at the left-hand edge.

Inks may also be subjected to security measures by the addition of visible fluorescence. Chemicals are added to the ink so that when the ink is subjected to ultra-violet light it fluoresces back a different colour.

Although there are many hundreds of firms that have been involved with security printing over the last few centuries, it would be impossible in the space available to give details of them all. It is for this reason that we will look at only three major companies, and that is because they are still in existence today. These companies are De la Rue, Bradbury Wilkinson and Company Limited and the American Bank Note Company.

I should, however, like in passing, to mention a few of the other companies that have produced some very beautiful work and these will be covered to some extent by the captions on the illustrations. Lizars, Batho and Bingley, Barclay and Fry, Blades East and Blades, and Skipper and East are all British companies that produced most of their work in the nineteenth century. Giesecke and Devrient is a German company which is also worthy of mention because of their beautiful underprint work.

De la Rue

It was in the hamlet of Le Bourg on Guernsey in the Channel Islands that Thomas de la Rue was born in 1793. Thomas was one of eleven children and when the family sold their farmhouse in 1802 and moved to St Peter Port the family had no planned future for him. However, in 1803, still just at the age of nine he began a seven-year apprenticeship to learn the art of printing. In 1811 and with his apprenticeship over, Thomas started as editor of a newspaper formed with the backing of another man, Tom Greenslade. By 1812 they were producing a weekly newspaper but because of their temperaments the association was not to see the year out. At the age of nineteen Thomas started his own paper and married Jane Warren, a Devonshire girl he had met during his partnership with Greenslade. In 1815 Thomas handed over his paper to his brother-in-law and shortly afterwards left for England.

At the age of twenty-five Thomas was to be found in London registered as a straw hat manufacturer, but by 1828 there is clear evidence of a diversification of interest away from the production of hats when, from his experiments into the production of paper and dyes, he developed an interest in playing cards. In 1830 Thomas formed a partnership in a stationery business which also produced playing cards and by 1831 he registered, for duty purposes, his first ace of spades. In 1835 the partnership ended and, having moved into new premises at 110 Bunhill Row in the City of London, Thomas started a new life founding his dynasty. From this year until 1838 the company did not prosper, but after a lot of financial difficulties which nearly destroyed the firm Thomas came back from the brink and produced a commemorative copy of the *Sun* newspaper for the coronation of Queen Victoria. It was a sell-out. A great deal of credit for Thomas's revival must be given to his son Warren who was a great friend of Charles Button, one of Thomas's largest creditors, and in 1837 Warren became a partner. In 1840 Thomas finally embarked on his *true forte,* security printing. Through Warren's friendship with Edwin Hill he met his brother Rowland who was responsible for the introduction of the prepaid Penny Postage. Although De la Rue started by printing envelopes, by the 1860s they were producing postage stamps. In 1858 Thomas retired from the business, leaving Warren and William (Colonel Billy) de la Rue in charge. In 1858 came a real turning point for De la Rue when they were granted a great deal of work, at the expense of Perkins Bacon, by the Crown Agents. In this same year De la Rue became rivals of Perkins Bacon by winning the contract to produce banknotes for Mauritius. This was De la Rue's first venture into this type of work and it was carried out by copperplate printing. De la Rue went from strength to strength, producing amongst other things the Confederate Stamps for which they were never completely paid. In 1870 Colonel Billy died and Warren took control, signing up his two eldest sons Warren William and Thomas Andros as partners. In 1880 Warren retired and died in 1889. In 1896 Warren William fell from a horse and seemed from then on to become even more eccentric than he had been before. It also seemed to herald a gentle forced retirement and Thomas Andros took over, and in 1898 De la Rue became a Public Company. Thomas Andros finally died in 1911 from the shock of losing the Inland Revenue account which he was asked to share, on the renewal of contract, with Harrisons.

Thomas Andros's eldest son Evelyn took over although his interest in the company was limited. A brief moment of glory came with the outbreak of the First World War when De la Rue designed and printed the Bradbury 1st series 10/– note. The £1 went to Waterlow Bros. & Leighton and for the second series the roles were reversed. Evelyn went to war and Ivor who succeeded him followed shortly afterward. The business was left in the hands of Stuart who carried on even after the other two returned. Albert Gronow, who was ex-Waterlow, now joined, as did Harold Rapkin on the condition that he brought key people from Waterlow with him. These men were shortly followed by a junior clerk Bernard Westall, who was to play a key part in the resignation of Stuart on a vote of confidence, after an action brought by De la Rue against Waterlow failed. The line of De la Rue ended with the exit of Stuart, and Sidney Lamett joined the board as chairman and managing director. Some reorganisation of the firm occurred and just when Bernard Westall was thinking of leaving he was offered the chance to represent the firm on a trip to Siam because they wanted to convert to printing by copperplate. Although not very experienced in this field Westall succeeded in securing both the contract and his future with the firm. It was a marvellous piece of business acumen. Using a rather flamboyant salesman called Albert Avramow, Mr Westall now acquired from Dr Kung, Minister of Finance at the Central Bank, a third share in a Chinese order for 90 million copperplate printed banknotes, with an additional order for 60 million notes thrown in for luck. When Dr Kung came to England for the coronation of George VI, De la Rue acted as PR for him and so secured an order for four issuing banks that totalled 800 million notes to the value of three million pounds. For De la Rue it put the final seal on their reputation as one of the finest security printers in the world.

Swedish Wenersborg Enskilda Banken 50 Kronor note, 1879. A printer's proof by Bradbury Wilkinson & Company.

Left above: A Waterlow & Sons publicity note produced in a banknote format in order to show the type of work they were able to produce.

Left below: Belgian Congo Banque Centrale 500 Franc note, 1 June 1959. The reverse of this De la Rue and Co. Ltd. specimen note.

Bradbury Wilkinson

William Bradbury was born at Bakewell in 1799 and after a period in Lincoln he came to London in 1824 to form a printing firm with his brother-in-law William Dent. In 1826 another partner called Manning joined the firm but this joint partnership did not last long, as four years later the company became Bradbury and Evans. This partnership was to last over forty years.
Henry Bradbury was born in 1831, the eldest son of William Bradbury and the most bril-

liant. His brother William Hardwick Bradbury, a year younger, also joined the family firm. At the age of nineteen Henry Bradbury was sent to study at the Imperial Printing Office in Vienna. On his return to England he had many new ideas to inject into the family business. Although there is no proof, because so many of Bradbury Wilkinson & Co. Ltd.'s archives were destroyed during the Second World War, it would appear that, although remaining on Bradbury and Evans' payroll, Henry formed his own company in 1856. Henry was quick to see the dangers that photography might have on banknote production and his second talk to the Royal Institution in 1856 covered 'The Security and Manufacture of Bank-Notes'. In 1860 he wrote a book called *Specimens of Bank-Note Engraving* which was published and printed by Bradbury and Evans. In 1860 when he was only thirty, Henry died, prematurely ending a brilliant career. On his death the company was controlled by William Hardwick Bradbury but he was really more interested in the publishing aspects of the firm.

The Wilkinson family came from Lincolnshire, and the fourth son of David Wilkinson was called Henry. He was born in 1795. Henry was trained in the printing business,

Banco de Espana 100 Peseta note, 1906. Printed by Bradbury Wilkinson & Company.

Cyfarthfa & Hirwain Iron Works 1 Guinea note, 1 April 1825. One of the most attractive notes of a British sundry issuers. Printed by Perkins & Heath from steel.

and his son Robert trained as a copperplate engraver. There is evidence that Robert was working with Henry Bradbury at the time of his death, hence the formation of Bradbury, Wilkinson & Co. in 1861, with the help of Bradbury and Evans' capital. In the early days of Bradbury Wilkinson & Co. Ltd. it would appear that banknote orders were executed using Bradbury and Evans plates. After a loss in the first year Bradbury Wilkinson & Co. Ltd. forged ahead as the predominantly South American-based business spread world-wide. In 1871 the Company received its largest order since its formation, that of six million notes for Uruguay. The order was delivered by the end of the year. In 1871 the company also started its first postage stamp work for the state of Hyderabad, but although they engraved the plates the stamps were printed locally. It was also in 1871 that Bradbury Wilkinson first started its association with the Crown Agents.

The American Bank Note Campany

The American Bank Note Company can trace its roots back to Robert Scot who in 1795 was living in Philadelphia. Scot was born in England around 1750 and came to live in Philadelphia in 1788. He became employed in the Mint there but retained his interest in banknote engraving. John Draper was an assistant of Scot and it was he who in 1810 teamed up with George Murray and Gideon Fairman to form the company Murray, Draper, Fairman & Co. We assume

American Chesapeake & Ohio Canal Company $10 note, 9 August 1840, with a central vignette of the signing of the Declaration of Independence (worth comparing with the current US $2 note). 'Medallion engraved' heads in centre and right edge. Printed by Underwood Bald Spencer and Huffy.

Scot did not join them because he was by now sixty and secure in his job at the Mint. With regard to the partners in this new found company, Murray was an English-trained Scotsman and Fairman came from Connecticut. The company progressed through many partnership changes at various times and several partners had much to do with the progression of banknote design. Two such partners were Asa Spencer, who invented the geometric lathe, and Jacob Perkins who invented transferring. Jacob Perkins was born in 1766 in Newburyport, Massachussetts. He trained as a gold- and silversmith and was extremely mechanically minded; by the age of twenty-one he was already submitting designs for coin striking machines. In 1790 Perkins married Hannah Greenleaf and their second daughter married Joshua Bacon in about 1814.

In 1818 the Society of Arts in London held an investigation into banknote design to try and prevent forgery; Perkins left America to attend this meeting in England and he took with him Fairman, Spencer and a native of his home town called Charles Toppan. The designs that they put forward were not generally appreciated but Fairman and Perkins stayed to form a company with Heath. Leaving Perkins behind, Fairman, Spencer and Toppan returned to America in 1823 and with the death of Murray reorganised themselves into another printing firm, called Fairman, Draper, Underwood & Co. In 1858 'The Association' known as the American Bank Note Company was formed, although this name had been used in conjunction with Jocelyn, Draper, Welsh & Co. as early as 1854. 'The Association' was formed from seven companies: Danforth, Perkins & Co.; Bald, Consland & Co.; Toppan, Carpenter & Co.; Jocelyn, Draper, Welsh & Co.; John E. Gavit;

Rowdon, Wright, Hatch & Edson; and Wellstood, Hay & Whiting. Of these different partners a little more should be said. Moseley Danforth started as an apprentice in the Hartford Graphic Banknote Engraving Company and when trained opened his own business in New Haven, Connecticut in 1821. In 1824 he moved to New York and joined Murray, Draper, Fairman & Co. in 1839. Nathaniel Jocelyn was a friend and co-worker of Danforth when they were in Hartford. Jocelyn formed Jocelyn, Darling & Co. in 1831 then worked with Toppan, Carpenter & Co. and Murray, Draper, Fairman & Co. before forming Jocelyn, Draper, Welsh & Co. John E. Gavit lived in Albany N.Y and succeeded the firm Hall, Packard & Cushman which he continued until 1858. In 1848 the firm Wellstood, Benson & Manks started and in 1855 became Wellstood, Hay & Whiting.

Ralph Rawdon lived in Cheshire until he started an engraving business at Albany in 1816. After several partnership changes the firm became New York-based in 1828 under the name Rawdon, Wright & Co. A mention should also be given to the Durand brothers. When Asa Spencer died in 1847 Cyrus Durand succeeded him as lathe engraver. He improved the design of many machines and broke the code by which Perkins had built his transferring machine. Cyrus also built himself a geometric lathe. Asher Durand, however, was more interested in design and he popularised the use of allegorical figures on banknotes and documents. From 1879 onwards more companies joined the American Bank Note Company to form the 'Consolidated Company'; these companies were Bradbury, Wilkinson & Co. Ltd. and the Western, the International, and the Franklin Lee Bank Note Companies. The Canadian Bank Note Company was added in 1896 and the present-day company finally took the form it is today in 1911.

The Canadian Bank of Commerce $10 note, 2 January 1917. Produced by the Canadian Bank Note Company but copyright of the American Bank Note Company.

The Norwegian government in exile contracted Waterlow and Sons to print
liberation notes in 1942. Only the two lowest denominations were ever used as
there was a new issue in 1944 of the high denominations, dated 1944 and with
the additional word 'Krigsseddel' (war banknotes). They were put into
circulation in northern Norway in the autumn of 1944. Withdrawn during the
currency reform of 1945, these issues are exceptionally rare.

4

Autographed Banknotes

Gold and silver have intrinsic value; paper money has only trust to depend on. For this reason the signatures that appear on paper money are of considerable importance. In normal times a printed signature would suffice but on many occasions it has been found necessary for distinguished people to apply their hand-written signatures to paper money in order to inspire trust and confidence.

Such practice was not confined to the early paper money of the world. Even as late as World War II there were occasions when hand-written signatures were needed. Such a case was the Ionian Islands, a group of seven islands in the Ionian Sea which were under Greek control when they were occupied by the Italians, who, eight days after setting up a 'Chief of the Political and Civil Affairs' began issuing paper money for the new régime. The inhabitants did not mind using the low denominations but they would not trust the high denominations of 500, 1000 and 5000 drachmas. The notes were issued in February 1942 and the Axis powers were obliged to allow the Royal Greek Crown to be overstamped on the notes which were then hand-signed by Vassilios Rapolikas, a well-known and trusted Greek military commander. The notes then circulated until September 1943 when the Ionian Islands came under Allied control and they were retired from circulation.

Hero of the Norwegians, Major General W. Steffens, had no time to hand-sign emergency notes, but the people accepted his photostat signature when, encircled at Voss near Bergen, he issued his own siege notes after telephoning the Norwegian Bank at Bergen for permission to do so. His forces were able to hold up the Axis advance just long enough for the king and his ministers to board a British destroyer and form a government in exile in England.

Mr R. G. Garrett, manager of Fanning Island Plantation, Ltd, is responsible for some of World War II's most valuable paper money. Fanning Island was a relay station of the Cable and Wireless Company and an Allied task force was hurriedly sent there to maintain the vital communications link between Australia and the United States. The small amount of coinage that sufficed for the needs of the plantation workers was quickly used up when American sailors and soldiers got their hands on it. Mr Garrett managed to get a plane to Honolulu and there had special banknotes printed with the wording 'One pound Australian currency redeemable only at the office of the Company at Fanning Island'.

As the need for small change subsided the notes were cut in half and used as cinema tickets – for on war-time Fanning Island there was a shortage of everything. Some halves were marked in blue pencil, and others in red, to represent different priced seats. The result was that less than 20 complete notes are now known to exist. They bear the signature of Mr Garrett.

One signature very popular with collectors is that of Mr E.L.Hoffien, manager of the Anglo Palestine Bank. He achieved what in normal banking circles was considered the impossible. It was clear to the Israelis that the British intended to leave Palestine, over which they had mandatory status, in a state of chaos. Israel needed its own banknotes. Mr Hoffien travelled to the USA and negotiated with the American Banknote Company to print them. There were very difficult problems. The American Banknote Company could not, under international law, print banknotes for a country which already had its own banknotes – the Palestine Currency Board notes issued under the auspices of a sovereign state.

Mr Hoffien persuaded them there was a way round the problem. The legal tender clause, which appears on early proofs of the notes, 'The bank will accept this note for payment in any amount', was changed on the actual notes to the meaningless words: 'The bank will accept this note for payment in any account'. Also, it was necessary to use denominations of 'Palestine Pounds' although the new currency was, of course, to be Israel Pounds. Getting the notes printed was only one problem; now Mr. Hoffien had to deliver them. The only Israeli airport Lod was in Arab hands. A temporary airfield was set up in the north of Israel and the notes were delivered by the Royal Dutch Airlines, and transported by armoured cars to the vaults in Tel Aviv. On 17 August 1948 the Bank Note Ordinance Act by the Israeli Parliament was passed and the very next day, to the surprise of those officials who anticipated financial chaos, the new notes were put into circulation.

As a precautionary measure the 'Jewish National Authorities' had been hoarding the British issues, the Palestine Currency Board notes, and these were now returned to the Crown Agents for redemption.

In doing so they created one of the rarest notes in the world, the £100 Palestine Cur-

rency Board note which has fetched more than £7000. Although shrouded in mystery, the story is that the insurance for the shipment of notes was so high that the authorities resorted to the simple expedient of tearing the notes in halves and sending them by separate shipments, thus avoiding high insurance costs. Whatever the truth may be, the fact is that only a handful of complete £100 notes have survived.

For a time the Israelis had more pressing problems of a military nature to resolve, but once able to give more attention to its banking system, they replaced their first issue of notes with the Bank Leumi Le-Israel, which now carried normal banknote wording. However, such was the rush with which it was all done that the American Banknote Co. refused to place their name on the notes because of the bad quality printing which had been forced on them by the hurried delivery.

Perhaps the most unusual signature on a banknote is that of the famous revolutionary, Ernesto Guevara, an Argentinian who was second in command to Dr Fidel Castro when he took over Cuba in 1959. Made president of the National Bank in 1960 Che Guevara did something no banking house had ever done before, he signed the banknotes with his nickname only, 'Che'. When the Western powers broke off diplomatic relations with Cuba in 1961, Castro responded by issuing a decree on Saturday 5 August of that year, invalidating all circulating notes on the following Monday, 7 August. All those who had left Cuba with millions of *pesos* in Cuban currency were ruined overnight. Only 'Che' notes were valid.

Colonial American signed notes

The richest harvest for autograph collectors in the paper money world comes from the early colonial issues of America. Early colo-

'Che' Guevara became president of the National Bank of Cuba in 1960 and signed the notes with his nickname 'Che' – the only bank president in history to do so. The reverse of the note depicts warlike scenes of Fidel Castro's guerilla troops.

nists were starved of gold and silver and, in most cases, forbidden to issue paper money. With the Revolution notes were issued in profusion and all carried the hand-written signatures of famous Americans.

Among the signers will be found the names of nine men who were also to sign the Declaration of Independence. They are: Abraham Clark, George Clymer, William Ellery, John Hart, Francis Hopkinson, Philip Livingston, John Morton, George Walton and James Wilson.

There is still much research to be done on these early signatures, and historians have traced a number of delegates to the Stamp Act Congress of 1765 on early notes: Joseph Borden, Metcalfe Bowler, Hendrik Fisher, Christopher Gadsden, Philip Livingston, Robert R. Livingston, Leonard Lispenard, Thomas Lynch, John Morton and John Rutledge.

Some of the signatories to the United States Constitution (1787) also signed notes: John Blair, David Brearley, William Few, Nicholas Gilman, William Jackson, Thomas Mifflin, Charles Pinckney, Charles Cotesworth Pinckney, Edmund Randolph, John Rutledge, James Wilson. Other signatories of the Articles of Confederation (1777) can be found and many of the important American families can trace their ancestors to these pioneering notes of the United States – although the earlier notes were headed 'United Colonies' before the final break was made.

The Continental Currency which was to give rise to the expression 'Not worth a Continental', was too large an issue for important statesman to be able to devote the time to hand-sign. So they appointed 275 people to sign the currency for them. Among these signatories is one of particular fame: Lieutenant John Mease of Washington's army. American forces stealthily crossed the Delaware above Trenton and, on Christmas Day, surprised and routed the British who, dulled by Christmas celebrations, assumed from the camp fires across the river that the American army was resting and celebrating as well. But in fact Lieutenant Mease was the officer in charge of the detail whose job was to keep the camp fires burning brightly to fool the British.

While not signers of notes, two very well-known Americans were connected with them. Paul Revere, one of the world's greatest silversmiths, took time out to design notes for the revolutionaries including the famous 'Sword in Hand' issue which shows a Minute-man with drawn sword and the words 'Issued in defence of American Liberty'. Benjamin Franklin printed paper money and his name appears on the backs of many Delaware notes. He also invented the marble paper used on early Continental issues.

As America grew in stature and expanded into the Wild West, banks followed the pioneers. It is said that more than 9000 banks issued paper money, much of it very colour-

£6 New Jersey note of 1776, on mica flaked watermarked paper, with decorative border by David Rittenhouse, who was to become the first Director of the United States Mint, in 1792. The signatures are interesting: Robert Smith, Judge of the Court of Common Please, Jonathan Johnston and John Smith; the latter founded the Philadelphia Hospital and organized one of the first Fire Insurance Companies in the US. In 1761 he was made a Commissioner for the trial of pirates.

ful and pictorial and reflecting the pioneering days with pictures of Red Indians, cowboys and plantations. Today the vast majority of these notes are known among collectors as 'broken banks' or 'wildcats'. Most of the banks went bankrupt. The wildcat banks often contain signatures of the infamous gangsters of the time. They would set up a bank in a ramshackle hut in the backwoods miles from the nearest community. Then, by bribery, they would make the local saloons give change in their currency notes. If the recipient ever traced the bank he would find the owners had gone 'like a wildcat'.

Of course some of the banks were very sound and have today been absorbed by the giant Insurance companies of America. Signatures on these notes are of the pioneer bankers of modern America.

Brigham Young, the famous Mormon, also signed paper money and there is a variety of different notes issued at Salt Lake City, most of which are very rare today and much in demand.

Siege notes

During the Siege of Mafeking Colonel Robert S.S. Baden-Powell – later to be Lord Baden-Powell and founder of the Scout movement – caused notes to be issued. There were problems as Baden-Powell recorded: 'We tried various dodges, drew a design on copper, bit it out with acid all right, but could not get sufficient pressure to print it though we tried it through a mangle, then we cut a croquet mallet in half and made a woodcut'.

In fact Baden-Powell drew the picture himself of a soldier with a field gun and another soldier with a Maxim, which was finally used for the 10s notes. They bear the wording 'Issued by authority of Col. R.S.S. Baden-Powell, Commanding Frontier Forces'. The first issue contained a spelling

Paul Revere was responsible for the famous little picture of the 'Sword in hand Minuteman' which appeared on American revolutionary notes in 1775. The inscription 'Issued In Defence of American Liberty' together with a copy of the 'Magna Carta' shows the strength of feeling at the time.

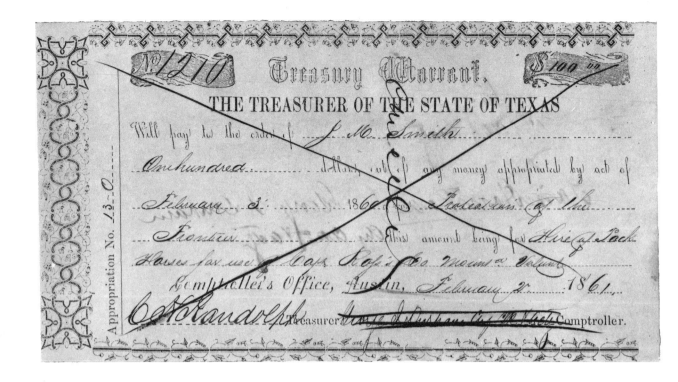

Will pay to the order of J. M. Smith
One hundred dollars out of any money appropriated by act of
February 3: 1860 Protection of the
Frontier this amount being for Hire of Pack
Horses for use of Capt. Ross Co Mount'd Volun''
Comptroller's Office, Austin, February 2''. 1861.
C. A. Randolph Treasurer Comptroller.

mistake, the word 'Commanding' being printed with the 'd' missing. The £1 note shows a picture of the home-made gun 'Wolf' (Baden-Powell was nicknamed by the natives the 'Wolf that Never Sleeps'), and was printed by the Ferro Prussiate process which was slow and enabled only twenty a day to be produced. These notes were hand-signed by Mr R. Urry of the Standard Bank of South Africa, and Captain H. Greener, the Chief Paymaster.

These notes were so popular as souvenirs of the siege that within days of the Relief of Mafeking the local paper was advertising sets, which comprised £1, 10s., 3s., 2s., and 1s. for £17 10s.

The hand-written signature of General Gordon appears on siege notes of Khartoum. At one stage experiments were carried out with printed signatures to save General Gordon the time-consuming job of signing, but these were not acceptable and although much rarer than the signed notes are not so popular among collectors who prefer the

Sam Houston, the 'father' of Texas, hand-signed Treasury warrants in 1861. His hand-written name also appears on many Texas issues in neat copperplate writing – but it was the work of his secretary who was authorized by Congress to sign on behalf of Houston.

actual signature of General Gordon. In his journal the General refers to paper money: 'I offered in paying three months 'Backsheesh' to the troops, to give orders for bulk sums, £120, £130 but they refused to accept them, they want regular paper money so I have issued £10,000 more... In this paper money I am personally responsible for the liquidation and anyone can bring action against me, in my individual capacity, to recover the money, while in the orders it might be a query whether they (Cairo authorities) might not decline to pay...'

His concern was justified. After Khartoum had been put to the sword the authorities in Cairo did try to avoid redeeming the notes and several civil actions were taken to get notes redeemed. The Mahdi declared that anyone found in possession of Gordon notes would be executed and it seems that no one was prepared to risk his life for a one piastre note which is today rarer than the rest of the eleven-denomination set put together.

Signed notes from the French Revolution

Many hundreds of different signatures can be found on these notes. It appears that everyone wanted to sign the notes – for on at least one issue there can be found over a hundred different signers, though there is only one signature per note.

Known as 'assignats' they were the brain-child of John Law (*see* also Chapter 5) who had been dead for some time when the revolutionaries introduced his system based on

10,000 francs note of the French Revolution, the highest denomination issued by the revolutionaries. The collapse of the assignat system which led to ruin and misery culminated with a public ceremony at which the plates were destroyed and hoards of paper money burned.

Early assignats of the French Revolution were interest-bearing and bore the portrait of Louis XVI. Known as 'Royal Assignats' they contributed to the king's downfall as he was identified from his portrait on such a note as he tried to escape from Paris.

land-backing of notes rather than metal backing. The church property and lands had been confiscated and were ideal for the purpose. John Law had been something of a financial genius seventy years previous to the assignat and, once being permitted to open a bank of his own, the Banque Générale, he made his notes redeemable in a fixed weight of coins. The French king had been accustomed to change values by royal edict to suit his purse; and Law's new bank with its fixed weight of exchange brought instant success and renewed business with countries overseas. The Duke of Orléans supported Law as his ideas became even more grand. He was to obtain the tobacco monopoly of France, and the monopoly of the tax farm. His scheme for the Mississippi Company was audacious in the extreme when one considers that Louisiana was then an unknown territory containing only a few trading posts. But with this he offered nothing less than the conversion of the national debt, offering 1500 million *livres* at 3 per cent to the State, intending to raise the money by selling shares in the company. Law, using much subterfuge, persuaded people to buy shares and the dealings on the Rue Quincampoix reached such a pitch that at one time in 1719 there were 30,000 foreigners in Paris all seeking to make fortunes. Many did, and the word 'millionaire' came into being. Law's power grew to such an extent that the English ambassador in France was recalled because he made the mistake of offending John Law. Edinburgh, where once Law had been sentenced to death for killing his adversary in a duel over a woman, now gave him the freedom of the city. On 5 January 1720, Law was made Comptroller General of France, but he was soon to topple from his pinnacle of success. Blocks of shares were put on the market and the value of the notes began to fall. Law introduced some desperate measures to save the situation, making paper at a 5 per cent premium over coin and, when that failed, simply forbidding the use of gold or silver for the payment of debts. But these measures stemmed the tide only for a few days and in October of 1720 John Law fled France and his notes were declared invalid.

With such a history it is perhaps surprising that the French revolutionaries so readily introduced the assignats, but on 19 September 1789 the National Assembly went ahead. First issues were interest-bearing and had the portrait of Louis XVI in the centre. It showed that, at that time, it was not the intention of the revolutionaries to execute the king – but it also led to his downfall in that it was from his portrait on one of the assignats that the king was recognised as he fled Paris.

At this time many towns and villages issued their own notes called *billets de confiance*. Clubs and societies also issued them, including the Jacobins. So far none of the famous names of the Revolution has been recognised among the signatories but there is still much research to be done.

Famous signatures on banknotess

Some famous men of history issued notes in exile with a view to raising money for their cause. Such a man was the great Hungarian patriot, Louis Kossuth. He hand-signed the high denominations of his American issues which are extremely rare though the small denomination notes are worth only a pound or two. His English issue is exceptionally rare because the British Government had them collected and burned after the Austrian Ambassador threatened to leave the country over the matter. Indeed Lord Palmerston's generous reception of Kossuth was made one of the charges of independent action which led to his dismissal in 1852. Nicaraguan notes can be found with the hand-written signature of William Walker.

Lajos Kossuth, Hungarian patriot, champion of liberty and President of the first Hungarian Republic (1848–1849), was driven from Hungary and issued notes in England and the United States to raise money for a return from exile, confident that he would receive revolutionary support. The revolution never happened. Some of the high denomination notes he issued have his handwritten signature on them.

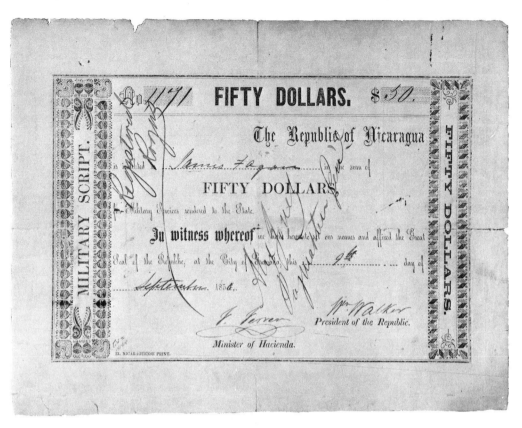

Military note of the Republic of Nicaragua for $50, dated 1856. William Walker (signature bottom right) was an adventurer who conquered Nicaragua with a small band of mercenaries. He ended up in front of a firing squad.

He was a US adventurer (1824–1860), who, in 1855, landed in Nicaragua with a mere 56 followers, seized a steamer on Lake Nicaragua and surprised and captured Granada, making himself master of the country. While Patricio Rivas was made president, Walker kept the real power by making himself commander of troops. He was soon in trouble and fought off a coalition of Central American states led by Costa Rica until 1857 when he surrendered to the United States Navy to avoid capture by the Central Americans. President James Buchanan personally ordered his release and in 1860 Walker was back in Central America, land-ing in Honduras. But this time he was arrested by Captain Salmon of the British Navy who handed him over to the Honduran authorities. They promptly put him in front of a firing squad on 12 September 1860, and ended his turbulent career.

Robert Owen, the great reformer, hand-signed some of his early notes which were meant to revolutionise the financial world, for they were for hours worked instead of sterling. A man would receive a ten-hour note and be able to buy goods to the value of ten hours' work. His system collapsed but it is much to his credit that he personally paid all the debts.

Famous signatures can be found on many common notes: the little *notgeld* (emergency town issues) of Germany include those of Cologne signed by the then Mayor, Dr Adenauer. Garibaldi, the hero of Italy, hand-signed many notes of the period of unification. Mazzini also issued notes bearing his signature.

Another area of signature-collecting on paper money is where great men have signed notes as souvenirs. Often the first few notes with low serial numbers of a new type of note would be presented to VIP's and one can find such notes hand-signed by the recipient, such as Winston Churchill, Baden-Powell, and in World War II, Eisenhower. Whole platoons, or bomber crews, would hand-sign notes as souvenirs for each other. The collector looks carefully at the signatures: one never knows, a famous person might be among them.

Robert Owen, publisher of Crisis in 1832, developed the idea of co-operation and a system of finance based on hours worked. He opened the London Exchange Bazaar which operated from 1832 to 1834 and commodities were sold and exchanged on this principle. Special valuers worked out the value of raw material used and time in making articles to give a 'labour hours' value. The system failed. Early notes of the Bazaar were hand-signed by Owen as 'Governor'.

This early and attractive lottery bond, depicting scenes of the operations of the Red Cross, was issued in 1882 by the Austrian Red Cross Company under the patronage of the Emperor and Empress of Austria. The company raised a loan of 6 million Austrian Gulden, divided into 600,000 bonds for 10 Gulden each, to be redeemed within fifty years. Instead of bearing interest, the bonds were drawn in an annual lottery for early redemption and winnings.

5 Getting to know old Bonds and Shares

Introduction

Collecting old bonds and shares, or 'scripophily', to use the newly-coined definition which has been accepted by the *Oxford English Dictionary,* is a fairly recent activity that has rapidly developed a strong following in Europe and America from an initial group of dedicated collectors in Germany. Now, on both sides of the Atlantic, a growing number of enthusiasts – already able to become affiliated to scripophilist clubs – subscribe to periodicals exclusively devoted to their hobby and obtain material from specialised dealers. This new, still largely uncharted and little-researched collecting field offers great scope for exciting discoveries. Until recently, there existed practically no literature on scripophily, but with the publication of the first catalogues of Russian railway bonds, Chinese and Confederate States bonds, identification and detection of the desired issues have at last become a simple and easy operation for collectors, which greatly contributed to the popularity of these categories.

The bonds and shares avidly collected by scripophilists do not belong to the kind that make up stock exchange indexes. Indeed, considered as obsolete or worthless securities in terms of stock exchange investment, they are, with a few exceptions, no longer traded by stockbrokers on the world exchanges. As relics of former, once perfectly valid, investments their value now resides in their intrinsic visual attractiveness, their history and their scarcity. Through some cruel quirk of fate, such once-valuable documents have at some time in history been turned into 'valueless' bits of paper. In the case of government bonds, wars and revolutions were mainly responsible for making countries default on previous obligations. New governments, striving to build fresh foundations out of the smouldering rubble and bring order and stability after chaos, have repeatedly proved reluctant to acknowledge the debts of a former régime. When the political map of Europe was redrawn after the First and Second World Wars, some countries disappeared altogether as independent states, while new ones were formed. With the ebb and flow of successive economic cycles, when a period of boom and expansion is followed by one of depression, companies have been created, have expanded and often merged, or, falling victim to the prevailing ill winds, have become insolvent. Defunct bonds and shares represent the testimonies of the vicissitudes of the economic and financial world. As socio-economic and historic exhibits of the capitalist age, they are of undisputed interest and value. However, to acquire a tangible piece of the economic or industrial history of a country is but one motive that spurs collectors. The graphic beauty of some of the certificates constitutes a sufficient criterion of desirability for many, while others are attracted to old

This 500 Francs, partly-paid bearer share was issued in 1880 by the Compagnie Universelle du Canal Interocéanique de Panama, a company established in the same year by Count Ferdinand de Lesseps, the promotor of the Suez Canal, in order to build a canal across the Isthmus of Panama. Contrary to the visionary picture of a ship sailing through the canal, over which the reclining female figures representing North and South America are joining hands, the French company never completed the construction despite a colossal capital injection in the project. It was defeated by sharply escalating costs and the ravages caused by yellow fever and malaria among the canal workforce and went into receivership in 1888. A new company replacing the first lived until 1904, when all concessions pertaining to the canal zone were sold to the United States.

bonds and shares because of the interconnection with other hobbies such as collecting stamps or banknotes. In this context, experts have discovered a number of examples where the same firms that engraved banknotes also printed bonds and shares, in some cases even using identical designs for the vignettes. As many government bonds carry fiscal stamps which form an already well-researched branch of philately, this in turn has attracted the interest of stamp collectors. The signatures found on bonds and shares can also form the basis of a collecting theme, as certificates of the same issue and denomination can show differing signatures.

Beyond their immediate appeal to collectors, old bonds and shares, with all they represent, constitute part of the cultural legacy of the western world, not only for their primarily historical relevance, but also for the variety of interests covered and the vast subject encompassed, which together are bringing scripophily into the focus of attention.

Right: Printed by the London firm of engravers Bradbury, Wilkinson & Co. Ltd., this beautiful bond depicting a view of Genoa Harbour forms one of a total of 6000 that were issued in 1913 by the Genoa & District Water Works Co. Ltd. which was first registered in 1912. Already in 1919, the company went into voluntary liquidation and the whole undertaking was sold for 2.5 million Lire.

Left : This bond for £100 issued by the Madeira-Mamoré Railway, a company incorporated in Maine, USA, in 1907, was printed by the London firm of Waterlow & Son. In 1931, having ceased its operations, the company handed over to the Brazilian government the railway it owned in the country. With no other assets to be realised, the company was deemed valueless in 1948 after the bondholders received a final payment of £146 shillings per £100 nominal of stock.

Many colonial issues are noted for their high pictorial quality. A representative example of these attractive certificates, this French bearer share, printed by Charles Skipper & East, was issued by the Société Coloniale de Plantations et Cultures à Madagascar, a company originally formed in Paris in 1914 with a capital of 300,000 Francs, divided into 3000 shares of 100 Francs. The certificate illustrated here was issued following a slight name change in the company in 1927. No dividend was paid out. (Detail)

How bonds and shares evolved

The system whereby other people's money helps to finance a particular venture is the chief characteristic of capitalism. The principle of dividing the financial burden among a group of individuals or corporate bodies, which would share in the profits as well as losses according to their contribution, was a logical consequence of the division of labour, by which the various stages in the production chain were no longer controlled by a single individual. Capital to fund an enterprise was provided by groups not necessarily connected with the execution of the project but prepared to take a risk in the hope of making a profit.

Kings and other heads of state, finding that revenues from taxes were often insufficient to cover their needs, approached the public for direct loans. At first, the money was mainly utilised to finance costly wars, but later the borrowed sums were employed to create various state services. Eventually, one loan would be raised to repay a previous one, so that the state debt would be carried forward indefinitely.

In Great Britain the best known early examples of capital raised by a group of individuals in order to finance an enterprise of a private nature were the arrangements entered into by the merchant adventurers in the times of Henry VIII and Elizabeth I to furnish and equip ships intended to discover new lands and to establish trade. The earliest example on record is the first British chartered company, the Muscovy Company, formed in 1553 to discover 'the unknown lands in the North' in a challenge to the Hanseatic League's trade supremacy in the Baltic. Because of the inherent risks in an enterprise fraught with many unknown hazards, the agreements were valid only for the duration of one particular voyage, which might last several years. If the expedition was successful and the ship returned, its hold filled with valuable goods, each member of

This share certificate for £25, dated 4 August 1853, was issued by the Oriental Bank Corporation, first formed in Bombay in 1842 under the name of Bank of Western India. Having moved its headquarters to London in 1845, the bank changed its name to the Oriental Bank Corporation. The Royal Charter, loosely worded as 'to operate anywhere east of the Cape of Good Hope' – which included India, at that time the sole preserve of the East India Company – was granted in 1851 despite opposition from the East India Company anxious to safeguard its banking and trading monopoly in India and the Far East. By the 1860s, the Oriental Bank had become a flourishing and prestigious banking establishment in India and China. Its decline during the late 1870s was associated with the spread of the dreaded coffee disease that had ravaged Ceylon plantations since its first appearance in 1868, as much of the bank's funds were locked in coffee investment. The bank's failure was announced in 1884. Reorganised as the New Oriental Banking Corporation, it lasted until 1892 when it eventually had to close down.

Left: Created in 1906 to organise a system of railways in southern Brazil, the company who also held various investment interests in Brazilian public utilities and industrial enterprises, has been essentially a holding company since 1940, when the Brazilian government seized all its assets in the country. Only partial restitution has been made since 1946. The last phase in the paying-off of the company's assets began in 1978 with the offer of a final payment of £5.30 per £100 of bonds, for which the bonds must be surrendered to the paying agents who will cut them in half as a sign of cancellation.

63

COLQUITT STREET TONTINE.

SHARE No. *72*

This is to Certify, That *Mr. Wm. Lees*
is the Proprietor of the Share, No. *72* — in the
LIVERPOOL COLQUITT STREET TONTINE,
and that the same is duly entered in the Register Book
of the Proprietors. And that the Nominee in respect
of the said Share, is *Sarah Lees his Daughter*
aged 15 years —

Liverpool, *1 Jany* 1807

*N. B. On every Transfer this must be given up,
and another will be granted in the Name of the
Person purchasing;—But as there is a possibili-
ty that an Interest may be transferred, without
giving up the former Certificate, it is recommended to Persons purchasing (previously to
paying their Purchase Money) to ascertain
the Regularity of the Transaction, by a reference to the Register Book.*

J. GORE.

*This Colquitt Street Tontine share, registered in
the name of Wm. Lees, for the benefit of his
daughter, Sarah Lees (aged 15), was issued on 1
January 1807. It represents a late example of the
loan scheme devised by Lorenzo Tonti in the
seventeenth century, by which the surviving
subscribers to the loan capitalised on the death of
other bondholders.*

the syndicate received an equal share in the profits. In the case of failure, accident or worse disaster, the subscriber lost his total contribution to the capital stock.

By 1657, the East India Company, which had been established in 1599 to open up trade with India, felt sufficiently confident to allow subscriptions to its capital to be made in varying amounts on a permanent basis and to be fully transferable to third parties. This marked the beginning of modern investment methods on the Stock Exchange. As the principle of a common capital subscribed for in freely negotiable units proved its usefulness and became more widely established, an increasing number of companies were formed on a joint-stock basis. One of the most illustrious and successful, the Hudson's Bay Company founded in 1670, is today Britain's oldest chartered company still trading.

In the first quarter of the eighteenth century, joint-stock companies of many kinds had become so prolific and led to such abuses that legislation to regulate the system became necessary. The 'Bubble Act' which prevented joint-stock companies to be formed without a royal charter of incorporation was passed by Parliament during the 'South Sea fever' of 1720 to protect established enterprises from the competition of new, often rash and even unsound ventures which cropped up in the wake of the success of the South Sea Company.

The South Sea Company was formed in 1710 on a similar kind of charter to the one granted to the powerful East India Company which it wished to rival. The government offered the South Sea Company exclusive trade concessions in South America. In addition, combining both trade and finance, the company planned to take over part of Britain's national debt. At the onset £10 million of government debt were incorporated into its stock when it was founded. The government paid 5 per cent interest, the company's main source of revenue as the trade with South America failed to materialize.

A few years later, the South Sea Company decided to take over another £1.5 million of government debt. The conversion plan worked out profitably for the company which made a capital gain on the difference between the par value of the stock and its market price at the time of the conversion of government stocks into South Sea shares, Encouraged by this success, the directors developed an ambitious scheme to take over the whole of Britain's national debt, which amounted to over £50 million and was a constant source of worry for the government. Of the total, £30 million had been borrowed from the public and £20 million borrowed directly from the Bank of England and the East India Company. It was eventually decided not to absorb the debt owed to the Bank and the East India Company but to convert £30 million of public borrowing into South Sea stock. Proposals to this effect were put before Parliament in January 1720. The Bank of England in its turn submitted a similar counter-proposal but was outbid by the South Sea Company which agreed to pay the government a much higher fee than its rival for the privilege of converting government securities into South Sea stock. The whole success of the operation depended on the shares in the company standing above their par value. This was achieved by skilful propaganda and gifts of free stock to well-placed and influential persons. The 'South Sea Bill', authorising £30 million of government debt to be converted into South Sea shares, was passed in April 1720. The stock had already risen in anticipation from £128 to £300. This was to be only the beginning.

At exactly the same time as the South Sea boom was getting into full swing in England, France was thrown into the turmoils caused by the disintegration of John Law's 'Mississippi Scheme'. In August 1717, John Law, a Scot who had lived in Paris since 1713, formed a company called *Compagnie des Indes Occidentales,* better known as the Mississippi Company, whose purpose was to expand and develop all commerce between France and Louisiana, a vast and largely unknown colony in North America with a reputation of fabulous wealth. By a massive publicity campaign, the French authorities tried to encourage the colonisation of the new land; for the first time a French governor for Louisiana was appointed and the foundations of a new city, called New Orleans in honour of the Regent, Philippe, duc d'Orléans, were laid in 1717. Despite all these efforts, Mississippi shares were not doing particularly well, trading at only 300 *livres* in May 1719, against their par value of 500 *livres* (or £25).

Meanwhile John Law, as chief financial advisor to the Regent, developed his theories on credit to benefit the economy of the whole nation and improve the standard of living. During the two preceding years, implementing his plan of regulating France's economic structure, he had acquired control, on behalf of the Mississippi Company, of the entire colonial trade. In August 1719, it was announced that the Mississippi Company would take over the whole of the national debt amounting to 1,500,000,000 *livres* (or £75 million). In return for this sum which it was to receive, the French government would pay 3 per cent interest to the company and distribute the capital among the holders of government securities. In Law's own words, 'the intention of the company is that the creditors shall invest the money they receive (from the government) in the shares which are now offered to them at less than their value, thus they will be enriched while the State is relieved'. Mississippi shares doubled within a month and from then on climbed to vertiginous heights during the autumn and winter of 1719, reaching 10,000 *livres,* 13,000, 15,000 and occasionally 18,000 (£900).

Public frenzy was the main factor that sent the price rocketing. It was also fuelled by the massive increase in the money supply which created unprecedented inflation. Share transactions were effected in a small, narrow street in Paris, the rue Quincampoix which had been the traditional place for dealing in government securities. It became the centre for Mississippi speculation. The street was jammed with people from morning till dark, when the gates at either end were closed. Owners of houses along the street ran a thriving business renting out their property to brokers at exorbitant prices. A cobbler was reputed to have made a fortune by simply putting chairs in his shed and supplying speculators with pens and ink for a fee. People from all classes and all countries were attracted to Paris and flocked to the rue Quincampoix, eager to grasp the chance of making money. Lords and ladies, whose status as peers prevented them from engaging in any form of trade, would sit in nearby cafés and send their servants to execute their orders. A valet, who had received precise instructions to sell at 8000 *livres,* found a buyer at 10,000 but kept the difference, investing in the shares himself. A little later, he was able to sell at a vast profit and retire a rich man. Such stories of rags to riches were apparently not uncommon. For the first time in history, the less privileged classes could actually realise their dreams of getting rich. Wild with joy, the masses idolised John Law.

But, together with the fast rise in Mississippi shares, the cost of living was sharply increasing too. By the end of 1719, this trend led a far greater number of shareholders to sell their holdings in order to put the profits into 'real wealth' such as gold and property. In January 1720 the stock started to fall. As the price did not recover, Law, who had just been promoted to the post of Comptroller General of Finance in the first week of January, tried to stabilise the share price to stop people from turning their money into gold.

A series of edicts was issued during spring 1720 establishing banknotes as the sole legal tender, forbidding the wear of gold jewellery without permission, and penalising the hoarding of gold and silver. Mississippi shares were fixed at 9000 *livres,* but this attempt to stop the rot encouraged even more people to sell. In the end, all share speculations were forbidden in Paris and the rue Quincampoix was closed. On 21 May 1720, Law issued an edict proclaiming that in order to combat inflation and to reduce the cost of living, the currency would be devalued. This was the signal for the end. Because of mob riots, the edict was withdrawn within a week and Law removed from office.

In England however, speculating in shares had become the current craze in the spring of 1720. In London crowds besieged Exchange Alley, a narrow cobbled street in the City where brokers had their offices. In the wake of the South Sea Company's success, myriads of new enterprises had sprung up, much to the annoyance of the South Sea directors who naturally wished all the speculating money to be channelled into South Sea shares. During April and May 1720 alone, fifty new companies were launched with capital raised by public share subscription. As the weeks passed, the purpose of some of these ventures became more and more eccentric. At the same time as France's economic system was collapsing, the British were indulging in unbridled speculation.

From May till August 1720, the South Sea Company presented no fewer than four share subscriptions to the public and made two conversion offers to holders of government annuities. George I, a governor of the company since 1718, invested £20,000 in the first subscription in April which he quickly sold in June 1720 for £106,500. To encourage share purchases, only a down-payment of 10 per cent on the share value was required. Everybody in England, from the aristocracy to the lower classes, bought South Sea shares. Not to be left out, the Bank of England also adopted the policy of lending money on its own stock to see its share price rise. Occasionally voices of warning rose, but nobody heeded them. An anonymous satirist wrote in June 1720:

A wise man laughed to see an ass
Eat thistles and neglect good grass
But had the sage beheld the folly
Of late transacted in Change Alley
He might have seen worse asses there
Give solid gold for empty air.

At the end of August 1720 the South Sea share price, which had gone up ten times within a period of six months, began to fall as shareholders who had mostly bought on margin were forced to sell to meet their obligations. Having stood at £900 on 17 August, the stock had dropped to £190 by 28 September and became practically unsaleable during the autumn. The violence and suddenness of the crash surprised everyone, even the most virulent critics of the scheme. Panic selling and a run on the banks ensued. The whole country was in uproar and demanded punishment for the directors, who were sent for trial and stripped of their assets. The scandal extended to some members of the government and various peers.

The notion of credit, first developed and put into practice by John Law and abused by the South Sea Company directors, was so new at the time that it dazzled many investors. Writers of the day called it 'the new alchemy' and the 'mine of gold'. An early advocate of the South Sea Company, Jonathan Swift wrote in his *Journal to Stella* (November 1711) 'now I am resolved to buy £500 South Sea stock which will cost me 380 ready money'. By the end of 1720, having lost a vast paper fortune, the disillusioned Swift wrote this bitter stanza:

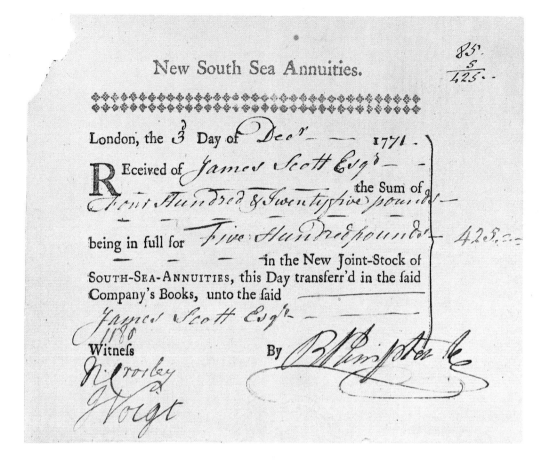

Formed in 1710, the company was entitled 'The Governor and Company of the Merchants of Great Britain trading to the South Seas and other parts of America, and encouraging the Fishing'. This inscribed stock receipt, dated December 3rd 1771, refers to the transfer of £500 of stock. The company's share certificates eventually disappeared after the government converted the outstanding capital of £10,000,000 into Consols in 1854.

As fishes on each other prey,
The great ones swallowing up the small,
So fares it in the Southern Sea,
The whale directors eat up all.

(*The South Sea Project*, 1721)

Defeated and discredited as a financial institution, the South Sea Company nevertheless survived until 1854 when Gladstone wound up its affairs and converted its remaining capital into Consols.

The results of the South Sea crash were not disastrous for the country, although many people lost money and public confidence was badly shaken. The 'Bubble Act' of August 1720, according to which all joint-stock companies had to be granted a royal charter to be allowed to trade, remained in force until the 1840s when a new Company Act was passed. Until then, partnerships were the most common type of trade association. Until the start of the boom in railway investments in the beginning of the nineteenth century, government stocks and a few public utilities were, by and large, the only securities traded. While the principles behind the Mississippi Company and the South Sea Company, precursors in the field, came ahead of their times, modern stock market methods developed with the progress of the industrial revolution which swept through Europe and North America from Britain at the beginning of the nineteenth century.

What are bonds and shares?

The common factor linking together joint-stock companies is that their capital is raised by shares. As well as bonds, shares are issued to the public by subscription. They form the

This share certificate for £1 was issued by The Great Ship Company, whose name refers to the steamship 'The Great Eastern', a replica of which appears on the company's seal. Designed by I.K.Brunel and built in London, the massive ship, five times larger than any vessel of that time, was launched in 1858 following three months of unsuccessful attempts that cost the lives of two workmen. During its short existence of barely thirty years, it proved a financial failure and ended up at the breaker's yard in 1888.

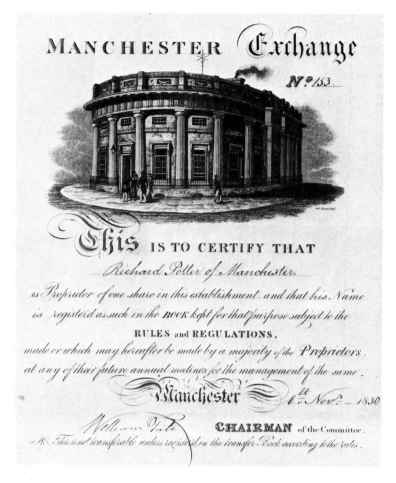

MANCHESTER Exchange

N° 153.

This IS TO CERTIFY THAT

Richard Potter of Manchester

is *Proprietor of one share in this establishment, and that his Name*
is *register'd as such in the BOOK kept for that purpose subject to the*
RULES and REGULATIONS,
made or which may hereafter be made by a majority of the Proprietors
at any of their future annual meetings for the management of the same.

Manchester ━━━ *6th Nov^r* 1830

CHAIRMAN *of the Committee*

N.B. This is not transferable unless register'd in the transfer Book according to the rules.

Begun in 1806, Manchester's second Exchange was called 'The Commercial Building', to be known as 'The Exchange' only well after its formal opening. The Company's original capital of £20,000 was raised by issuing 400 shares of £50 each which were all subscribed for within hours. The building was opened on 2 January 1809, numbering 1543 members whose annual subscription had been fixed at the 'steep' rate of two guineas.

Right: The Barcelona Traction, Light & Power Company was incorporated in Canada in 1911 to acquire and operate electric power and light as well as transport in Barcelona and the province of Cataluna. During the Spanish Civil War, a 'workers' committee' in 1936 seized the entire control of the company's business and assets. At the end of the war, in 1939, these were restored to the company which sought to re-establish the supply of electrical services. But, after the Second World War, the Spanish Provincial government declared the company bankrupt in 1948. Its foreign assets, mainly Canadian, were sold off by auction in Spain in 1952. This ruling however was challenged by the Supreme Court of Ontario whose findings were that the Canadian assets were represented in bonds and shares held in Canada.

company's stock capital. W. Thomson's *Dictionary of Banking* defines a share as being 'the right which a member of a company has to a certain proportion of the capital which, in its turn, is the total sum contributed by the members'. A bond, under the general meaning of the term, is 'a document under seal whereby a person or company binds himself, or itself, to pay a certain sum or to fulfil a certain contract'. The distinction between a bond issued by a private individual and that issued by a company or government is simply that whereas the former is not considered as a marketable security, the latter is openly traded on the stock exchange.

In Britain shares are registered, which means that they are issued to a holder whose name appears on the document and is entered on the company's register of shareholders. Foreign shares, particularly from Europe, can either be registered or issued to bearer. In this case, the full benefits of the share are automatically conferred on its holder, even though the share may have changed hands, as is the case when holding cash. Initially, British courts of law treated bearer bonds with suspicion and recognised as proper negotiable instruments only those bearer bonds issued in foreign countries and traded in Britain. But by the late nineteenth century bearer bonds issued by British companies were eventually also accepted. Bonds are issued for fixed amounts whereas shares can be purchased for any number.

With registered stock, the procedure entitling the holder to his portion of the dividends or interest, as the case may be, is straightforward enough. The company automatically sends to all the shareholders entered in its register the proportion of dividends due to them. In the case of bearer stock, each certificate carries a sheet of coupons resembling tickets, each one numbered and dated, upon production of which the holder is entitled to receive the due amount of interest from specified paying agents.

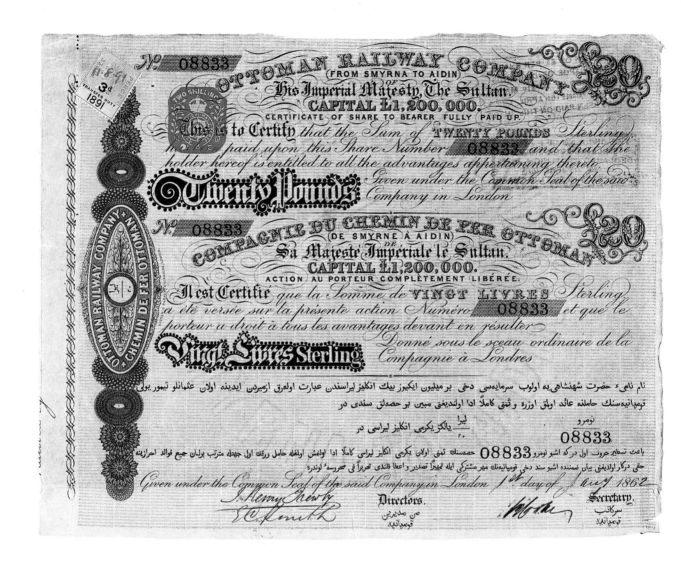

This £20 bearer share (Detail) was issued on 1 January 1862 by the Ottoman Railway Company established in London on 11 July 1856 under a fifth-year concession from the Turkish government to build the first railway in the country from the port of Smyrna to Aidin, a trade centre 80 miles inland. In return for the guarantee of a 6 per cent dividend on the shares and a number of interesting privileges to the company, the Turkish government was entitled to half the profits when the debt was paid off and the line's revenues exceeded 7 per cent. Construction began in 1858, with Lord Stratford de Redcliffe laying the foundation stone in Smyrna, and by December 1860, 27 miles were open. Obtaining additional concessions, the company increased its capital as early as 1861. Soon afterwards, it was troubled by serious differences with the Turkish government which, as from 1865, withheld payment of the dividend guarantee under the claim that the construction had not progressed according to the terms of the contract.

When all the coupons are exhausted, a fresh supply is obtained in exchange for the talon, a slip alongside the sheet of coupons attached to the bond.

Whereas in Britain the vast majority of certificates are registered in the name of their owners, a system which gives a tight control on stock ownership while at the same time affording greater protection to the holder in case of loss or theft, in Europe the ownership of bearer stock is quite common. One of the advantages of this system is that it is easily transferable and anonymous. Often, bearer certificates show an incomplete sheet of coupons. This is evidence of the certificate having been presented for collection of interest, when the agents effecting payment to the holder detached the coupon due. The remaining coupons were unclaimed, mostly because the security fell into default.

As a general rule, issued shares are documents on paper or sometimes on parchment stating the company's name, its capitalisation (the total sum subscribed for by shareholders) and the nominal value of the certificate – *i.e.* into how many units the capital has been divided. The document bears the seal of the company as well as one or more signatures by company officials such as a director and a secretary. Early share certificates show handwritten signatures in ink, while on later issues they are facsimile reproductions.

This share certificate, number 40, was issued on 19 July 1833 by the Herne Bay Pier Company, incorporated in 1831. The pier itself, constructed in 1831, was primarily intended a a landing stage. Taking the sea air on a ship cruise had become such a fashionable pastime that it was no longer befitting to let visitors in their elegant toilettes get wet on beach landings. The wooden pier which cost £50,000 to build only lasted until the 1860s and was replaced in 1873.

Unissued share certificates, which are sometimes found, never possessed any investment value. They are blank, without date, seal, signatures and stockholder's name – in the case of registered stock. Unissued certificates were held in reserve by the company to be issued as and when required to future investors of its shares.

In the case of bonds, the document indicates the title, the amount and interest rate of the loan, the name of the corporate body which raised it and the denomination of the certificate. An excerpt of the loan agreement often also appears, together with official signatures and seals, as well as government stamps.

A great number of old bonds and shares which come into the hands of collectors have been cancelled in one form or another to make them invalid as securities. The reasons for the cancellation are many and varied: it may have been the forced liquidation of a company, a merger with another, a name change or some other alteration in the company's structure, or perhaps a government repudiating a loan or reorganising it by exchanging the bonds for new ones. The certificates were called in and had cancellations stamped, punched or cut across them. In the case of British shares, these were simply withdrawn from the market and destroyed, which explains why old British share certificates are relatively rarer.

The interest in this cancelled certificate for 100 shares in the Mission Development Company lies in the facsimile signature of its world-famous President, J. Paul Getty. His company merged into Getty Oil on 30 September 1967. Each $5 share in Mission Development was exchanged for 1.6688 common Getty Oil shares of $4.

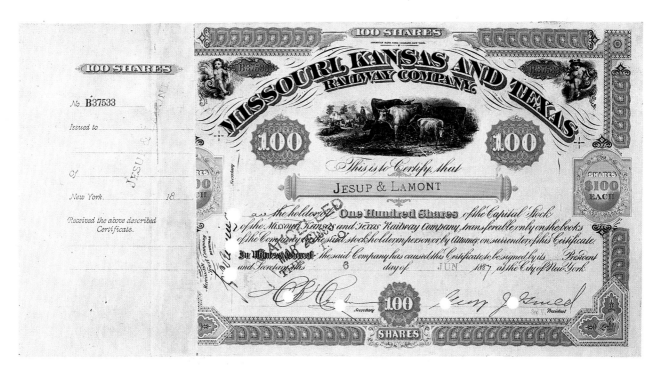

This share certificate depicting a rural scene with a herd of cattle browsing by a pond was issued by the Missouri, Kansas & Texas Railway Company in 1887 and bears the signature of its third vice-President, George J. Gould, the son of Jay Gould, the famous and ruthless railway stock manipulator who, after gaining control of the Erie Railway, set out to acquire a whole system of lines in the American South-West, in a bid to establish a Missouri-Pacific line. The Missouri, Kansas & Texas Railway, organised in 1870 by the consolidation of several neighbouring lines, was close to receivership when Gould acquired it in 1879. He implemented a policy of rate-cutting and hectic railway construction in the boom years between 1879 and 1881. This period was followed by a sharp decline and the shares were cancelled in 1890 when the company was reorganised.

Counterfeit bonds and forgeries

To deter the counterfeiting of bonds and shares, similar precautions were adopted as for banknotes. The same firms producing banknotes were employed to print bonds and shares, using very elaborate engraving methods and special paper and ink for printing. Nevertheless, there have been instances of contemporary forgeries, some of which were successful. Modern fakes of defunct certificates, however, are unlikely to occur because of the complexity and the cost of the process.

As an example, Criswell's *Currency Series,* vol. II lists a number of counterfeits of Confederate States bonds, even a completely bogus issue, which are all examples of contemporary forgeries made during the American Civil War. One particular counterfeit issue was apparently printed and sold outside the Southern States, as most of those that have turned up bear Dutch duty stamps.

Among famous forgeries committed, the one perpetrated in the early twentieth cen-

B-AKTIE

№ 716602

1 B-AKTIE   1 'B'SHARE

AKTIEBOLAGET KREUGER & TOLL

(KREUGER & TOLL COMPANY)

INCORPORATED ACCORDING TO THE LAWS OF SWEDEN

AKTIE KAPITAL 65.000.000 KRONOR   SHARE CAPITAL 65.000.000 KRONOR

AKTIERNA ÄRO FÖRDELADE I TVÅ SERIER, A-
OCH B-AKTIER Å NOM. 100 KRONOR, VILKA
AKTIER ÄRO LIKSTÄLLDA I ALLA AVSEENDEN
MED UNDANTAG AV ATT A-SERIENS AKTIER
MEDFÖRA EN RÖST, MEN AKTIER I SERIEN B
ALLENAST 1/1000 RÖST PER AKTIE.

THE SHARES ARE DIVIDED IN TWO SERIES "A"
AND "B" SHARES OF 100 SWEDISH CROWNS
EACH, AND RANK PARI PASSU IN ALL RESPECTS
EXCEPT THAT THE "A" SHARES CONFER ONE
VOTE PER SHARE BUT THE "B" SHARES ONLY
1/1000 OF A VOTE PER SHARE.

Administratie Maatschappy voor Algemeene Nyverheids Waarden

som tillfullo inbetalt beloppet för

EN

*B-aktie i Aktiebolaget Kreuger
& Toll med
100 kronor,
tillförsäkras härigenom mot-
svarande andel i bolaget i öfver-
ensstämmelse med lag och bo-
lagsordning.
    Med detta aktiebref
följa utdelningskuponger jämte
talong.*

having paid in full the amount for

ONE

*"B" Share of 100 Swedish Crowns
in the Kreuger & Toll Company
namely 100 Swedish Crowns
is registered as the Holder of the
said Share in the Company in
conformity with the Law and
the Articles of Association of the
Company. — Dividend coupons
and Talon are attached to this
Share Certificate.*

Stockholm, 1/7 1928.

AKTIEBOLAGET KREUGER & TOLL

tury by Ivar Kreuger, the 'Swedish Match King' is worthy of mention, if only because it remained undetected until after his suicide. From the modest match factory in Sweden which he had inherited, Ivar Kreuger built up a vast empire extending over several continents. With his reputation of turning whatever he touched into gold, his credit and that of his numerous companies was extremely good. Each year, the shareholders received very generous dividends, another ostensible sign that the companies were doing well. During the 1920s Kreuger granted a number of loans to various needy Central European governments. These were supposed to have been financed out of the vast profits of the Kreuger empire. In fact, far from that being the case, Kreuger had to borrow whole, or at least part, of the sums advanced. In one instance, the collateral he offered as security for the loan he requested was a bundle of Italian government bonds and promissory notes to a face value of $142 million, all forged and signed by himself. The bonds purported to be 6 per cent Treasury bills, with interest payable at Barclays' Bank, London, and dated Rome, 15 August 1930. Kreuger had ordered the lithographing of the bonds to be made by a Swedish firm that produced the shares for his own companies and was sworn to secrecy. Kreuger himself forged the signatures of the Minister of Finance and of the General Director. He must have been in such a panic that he spelt the minister's name in three different ways. The forged bonds were pledged as security by the International Match Corporation in New York against a loan to Italy.

Not technically counterfeits, but nevertheless illegal issues, were the shares printed by some of the more notorious directors of the Erie Railway Co., like Daniel Drew, Jay Gould and James Fisk, who resorted to unauthorised increases in the share capital of the company for their stock manipulations. As Vice-President of the Erie Railway,

Fisk had a steam-operated printing press installed in the basement of the Grand Opera House in New York, which became the site of the company's offices in 1868. Referring to it as 'the freedom of the press', Fisk used it liberally to flood the market with new shares, whenever he felt like it. In 1867 Commodore Cornelius Vanderbilt, in an attempt to gain control of the Erie Railway in order to incorporate it into his own New York Central system, tried to acquire a majority shareholding. As fast as his brokers bought the stock, new Erie shares were offered on the market. The notorious pair Fisk and Gould had been busy in the basement of the Grand Opera again, printing 100,000 new shares to a value of £10 million. Of the 150,000 shares he had purchased, Vanderbilt discovered that 100,000 were fictitious stock. The Stock Exchange declared them illegal and valueless. Meanwhile, Fisk and Gould had pushed the share price down by heavy short-selling (*i.e.* selling shares they did not have). When the shares halved in price, the two bought them back, thus retaining control and making a fortune for themselves.

Left: This share certificate was issued in 1928 by Kreuger & Toll, Inc., the company formed by Ivar Kreuger who became known as the Swedish 'Match King'. His worldwide empire, based on a number of exclusive match monopolies in several countries, collapsed after his suicide in Paris in 1932 when investigations into the affairs of his numerous companies revealed fraud and falsifications on a massive scale.

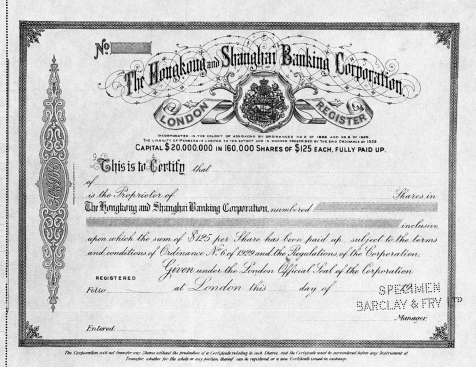

This rarely seen item is a specimen share, by Barclay & Fry Ltd., in the Hongkong & Shanghai Banking Corporation, which was originally formed in Hongkong in 1865 to cater specifically for the needs of the merchant community in China and the Far East. Very soon it assumed a leading role in arranging state and railway loans on behalf of the Chinese government.

Collectors' favourite Bonds

Among collectors, Chinese, Russian and Confederate States bonds have attained a special position of eminence. These three collecting fields are the only ones that have until now been researched and catalogued. In 1961, Criswell's *Currency Series,* vol II already featured Confederate and Southern States bonds in a descriptive listing, giving also rarity values. The book was published in the United States in Florida. For Russian and Chinese bonds, the two catalogues compiled by Drumm/Henseler in Germany on Russian railway bonds in 1975 and Chinese bonds in 1976 have become widely-accepted works of reference for collectors everywhere.

China

Chinese bonds, particularly, immediately attract the collectors' eye, not least because of their outstanding graphic beauty, their lovely vignettes in the oriental style and the intriguing and ornate Chinese characters. The history behind the various loan issues is itself fascinating and the research work already done shows that, contrary to common belief, far from being prolific, some of the Chinese bonds are very rare indeed.

Financial involvement of western powers with China began during the nineteenth century, when the manufacturing countries of the West looked upon China, a country still industrially undeveloped but densely populated, as a giant, virgin market for selling their industrial goods. Striving to tap this huge and unsophisticated market with seemingly limitless potential, Britain, together with other European countries, contrived to make China gradually accept trade with foreigners. Wary of external influences, China had for many centuries remained impervious to events and developments outside her empire. However, by the middle of the nineteenth century, China, already made vulnerable by decaying institutions and a weak government under the still ruling Manchu dynasty, could no longer effectively resist pressure from foreign powers. The most aggressive of these were Russia and Japan, closing in on her by land and by sea and extracting many concessions. Britain's opportunity to gain a foothold in this mysterious eastern country came with the 'Opium Wars' at the end of which China signed the Treaty of Nanking in 1842. It marked the end of China's isolation from the rest of the world and her forcible opening to the flow of western ideas and commerce. The treaty, which conceded the island of Hongkong to Britain, also provided for Canton, Shanghai and three other major sea-ports to become freely accessible to foreign merchants, who were allowed to settle in communities enjoying extra-territoriality under the jurisdiction of their own countries.

A succession of conflicts involving also

France, Germany, Russia and Japan, forced China to grant further concessions of territory. The last quarter of the nineteenth century saw Russia, following her policy of bringing Siberia and Central Asia under Tsarist rule, making firm inroads in the North in Manchuria, a very fertile province often referred to as the granary of China, and equally rich in mineral wealth. Meanwhile, the French had clashes across the border with Annam which they had taken from China. They nurtured an ambition to extend their colonial empire into Yunnan in southern China, whereas Germany, in a bid to establish a German colony in the Far East, claimed rights and concessions in the northern province of Shantung. Not wishing China to be carved up by these various powers, Britain, with the support of the United States, pursued 'the open door' policy, aimed at encouraging China to allow foreigners the right of free trade within the country.

Financial dependence on the West probably began in 1874 when the Hongkong and Shanghai Banking Corporation arranged to raise an 8 per cent loan of £625,615 for China. This was one among many others which were fully redeemed. In an effort towards industrialisation and modernisation of the country, China contracted a number of other loans between 1874 and 1894, which were mainly issued by the Hongkong & Shanghai Banking Corporation which quickly assumed a leading position in the handling of Chinese financial affairs.

The Sino-Japanese war of 1894–1895 which started with Japan invading Korea, was inspired by the urgency for Japan to set foot in mainland China before Russia completed the Trans-Siberian railway. The result of the war was a crushing and humiliating defeat for China. The Treaty of Shimonoseki forced China to make important territorial cessions to Japan as well as a heavy payment of war indemnity which amounted to £48 million. In addition, China also had to grant other major powers various territorial and trade concessions so as not to upset the balance of power within China. To pay the Japanese indemnity, China raised the capital first with the help of Russia through the Russo-Chinese loan of 1895 for 400 million francs which was placed in France but guaranteed by Russia. In an unofficial alliance between Britain and Germany, a second indemnity loan was arranged through a combination of the Hongkong & Shanghai Banking Corporation and the Deutsch-Asiatische Bank. Other Chinese loans raised under Anglo-German auspices include the 5 per cent Tientsin-Pukow railway loans of 1908 and 1910, issued in Britain by Chinese Central Railways Ltd. and in Germany by the Deutsch-Asiatische Bank.

By the turn of the century China had become heavily dependent on foreign powers to which she was deeply in debt. They controlled most of the railway lines, mines, ports and a great proportion of trade. With regard to railways, China was extremely slow and reluctant to accept the new mode of communication. China's first railway was a short line built from Shanghai to Woosung, a suburb of the town. Messrs. Jardine Matheson had obtained a concession for building a railway, with the express stipulation that animals only could supply the motive power. The company went ahead with the work, laying down a narrow-gauge 2 feet 6 inches railway which was completed in 1875. But, disregarding the terms of the contract, they introduced a steam locomotive amid violent protest from the local population. Still, no action was taken against the company to stop it from operating the railway which was often pelted with stones, until one day a Chinese labourer was hit and killed by an engine. The iron road had claimed its first victim in an accident in China, with the result that the British company's concession was cancelled and the operation of the railway suspended. In 1877 the Chinese government repurchased the line, had

This share warrant to bearer for 25 Shansi shares of £1 each was issued on 11 April 1906 by the Pekin Syndicate Ltd., a company first registered in London on 17 March 1897 with an issued capital of £1,540,000 for the purpose of obtaining and developing concessions for mines, railways and other industries in China. It acquired major concessions in the provinces of Shansi and Honan, where it built a railway for which the finance was raised in the 5 per cent Honan Railway Loan of 1905. The company traded as 'The Pekin Syndicate' until 31 October 1961 when its name was changed to 'Anglo-Continental Investment and Finance Company Ltd.'

the track torn up and shipped, together with the entire rolling stock, to Formosa, where today the islanders claim that they are in possession of the first Chinese railway.

Public acceptance of railways was slow and hard to obtain. Deeply superstitious and prejudiced, the population feared that the 'foreign devilroad' was desecrating the graves of their ancestors and turning the land sterile, while bargemen clamoured that the railways were ruining their trade. As from 1884, when China was at war with France over the Indochinese border and experiencing difficulties in sending troops to Tongking, the country's political leaders became increasingly convinced of the usefulness of railways, if at first only for strategic and military reasons. By 1887 the Empress Regent had approved the construction of a railway in China, from Taku to Tientsin, to facilitate the mobilisation of troops. This led to a stampede by foreign syndicates trying to secure concessions for mines and railways, backed by their respective governments.

However, the aggressive diplomacy by several foreign nations in occupying territories and seizing political as well as commercial privileges, the apparent loss of suzerainty by China as a result, and the subsidising of the country by foreign capital, all contributed to stir up a violent feeling of hostility against all foreigners in China. By spring 1900, in a climate of general economic hardship, these pent-up feelings of

resentment were released in an extraordinary outburst of violence which spread throughout the province of Shantung. Followers of the 'Boxer' movement, a kind of secret society whose aim was to drive all foreigners out of China, killed hundreds of Christian missionaries and thousands of their Chinese converts. At first unable or reluctant to repress the uprisings, the central government eventually gave its support to the Boxer cause and broke diplomatic relations with Western powers under the pretext that it could no longer vouch for the safety of the foreign communities in China. The assassination of Baron von Ketteler, the German envoy in Peking, marked the beginning of open hostilities in North China. The foreign powers sent an international relief force to Peking and Tientsin to rescue the diplomatic corps and the foreign settlements. The siege of the foreign legations in Peking lasted from 19 June to 14 August 1900. In Shantung, Canton, Shensi and the Yangtze provinces the order received from Peking to 'kill all foreigners' was altered by the local viceroys to 'protect all foreigners', but elsewhere in China foreigners and many Chinese Christian converts fared badly. On 14 August, the day the allied forces entered Peking, the Empress Dowager, disguised as a poor peasant woman, escaped in the early hours of the morning, taking the Emperor with her, and retreated to Sianfu to experience hardship and hunger. She remained there until September 1901, leaving her government to negotiate the best terms possible under the circumstances, with the foreign powers. On her return to the capital, she was received in triumph, apparently forgiven by everyone.

By the end of August 1900 when the rebellion was quelled, the Chinese government entered into difficult peace negotiations with the allied powers intent on imposing a heavy war indemnity. The amount of reparation China was eventually made to pay as a result of the Boxer Rebellion

Right: In order to finance the completion of the Shanghai-Hangchow-Ningpo railway and to construct a bridge over the Chien Tang River, the National Government of China raised a 6 per cent loan of £1,100,000, divided into 8000 bonds for £100 and 6000 bonds for £50, the latter being the rarer issue. The loan was to be secured on and paid from the revenues of the railway and 70 per cent of the income from tolls levied on the traffic over the Chien Tang river bridge.

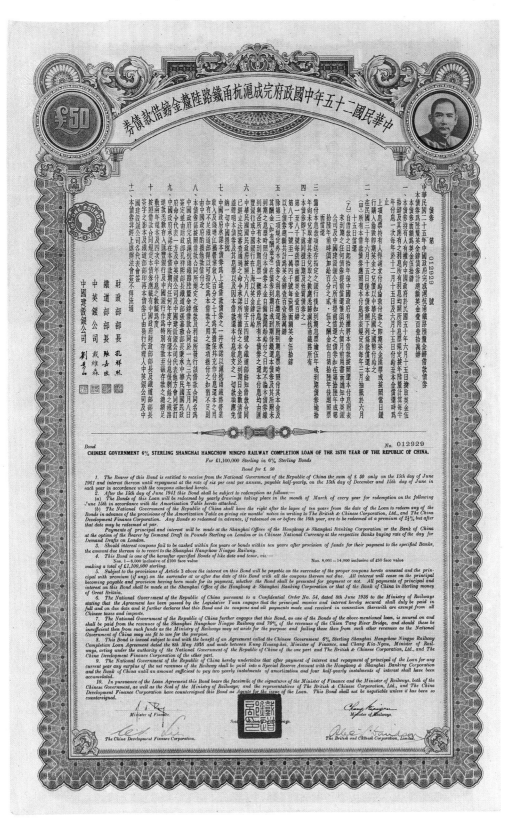

Bond No. 012929

CHINESE GOVERNMENT 6% STERLING SHANGHAI HANGCHOW NINGPO RAILWAY COMPLETION LOAN OF THE 25TH YEAR OF THE REPUBLIC OF CHINA.

For £1,100,000 Sterling in 6% Sterling Bonds

Bond for £ 50

1. The Bearer of this Bond is entitled to receive from the National Government of the Republic of China the sum of £ 50 only on the 15th day of June 1961 and interest thereon until repayment at the rate of six per cent per annum, payable half-yearly, on the 15th day of December and 15th day of June in each year in accordance with the coupons attached hereto.

2. After the 15th day of June 1941 this Bond shall be subject to redemption as follows:—

(a) The Bonds of this Loan will be redeemed by yearly drawings taking place in the month of March of every year for redemption on the following June 15th in accordance with the Amortization Table hereto attached.

(b) The National Government of the Republic of China shall have the right after the lapse of ten years from the date of the Loan to redeem any of the Bonds in advance of the provisions of the Amortization Table on giving six months' notice in writing to The British & Chinese Corporation, Ltd., and The China Development Finance Corporation. Any Bonds so redeemed in advance, if redeemed on or before the 16th year, are to be redeemed at a premium of 2½% but after that date may be redeemed at par.

Payments of principal and interest will be made at the Shanghai Offices of the Hongkong & Shanghai Banking Corporation or the Bank of China at the option of the Bearer by Demand Draft in Pounds Sterling on London or in Chinese National Currency at the respective Banks buying rate of the day for Demand Drafts on London.

3. Should interest coupons fail to be cashed within five years or bonds within ten years after provision of funds for their payment to the specified Banks, the amount due thereon is to revert to the Shanghai Hangchow Ningpo Railway.

4. This Bond is one of the hereafter specified Bonds of like date and tenor, viz:—

Nos. 1–8,000 inclusive of £100 face value Nos. 8,001–14,000 inclusive of £50 face value

making a total of £1,100,000 sterling.

5. Subject to the provisions of Article 3 above the interest on this Bond will be payable on the surrender of the proper coupons hereto annexed and the principal with premium (if any) on the surrender at or after due date of this Bond with all the coupons thereon not due. All interest will cease on the principal becoming payable and provision having been made for its payment, whether the Bond shall be presented for payment or not. All payments of principal and interest on this Bond shall be made at the Shanghai Office of the Hongkong & Shanghai Banking Corporation or that of the Bank of China in Sterling money of Great Britain.

6. The National Government of the Republic of China pursuant to a Confidential Order No. 54, dated 8th June 1936 to the Ministry of Railways stating that the Agreement has been passed by the Legislative Yuan engages that the principal monies and interest hereby secured shall duly be paid in full and on due date and it further declares that this Bond and its coupons and all payments made and received in connection therewith are exempt from all Chinese taxes and imposts.

7. The National Government of the Republic of China further engages that this Bond, as one of the Bonds of the above-mentioned loan, is secured on and shall be paid from the revenues of the Shanghai Hangchow Ningpo Railway and 70% of the revenues of the Chien Tang River Bridge, and should these be insufficient then from such funds as the Ministry of Railways may set aside for the purpose and failing these then from such other revenues as the National Government of China may see fit to use for the purpose.

8. This Bond is issued subject to and with the benefit of an Agreement called the Chinese Government 6%, Sterling Shanghai Hangchow Ningpo Railway Completion Loan Agreement dated 8th May 1936 and made between Kung Hsiang-hsi, Minister of Finance, and Chang Kia-Ngau, Minister of Railways, acting under the authority of the National Government of the Republic of China of the one part and The British & Chinese Corporation, Ltd., and The China Development Finance Corporation of the other part.

9. The National Government of the Republic of China hereby undertakes that after payment of interest and repayment of principal of the Loan for any current year any surplus of the net revenues of the Railway shall be paid into a Special Reserve Account with the Hongkong & Shanghai Banking Corporation and the Bank of China until an amount sufficient to pay two yearly instalments of amortization and four half-yearly instalments of interest shall have been accumulated.

10. In pursuance of the Loan Agreement this Bond bears the facsimile of the signature of the Minister of Finance and the Minister of Railways, both of the Chinese Government, as well as the Seal of the Ministry of Railways; and the representatives of The British & Chinese Corporation, Ltd., and The China Development Finance Corporation have countersigned this Bond as Agents for the issue of the Loan. This Bond shall not be negotiable unless it has been so countersigned.

Minister of Finance.   Minister of Railways.

The China Development Finance Corporation.   The British and Chinese Corporation, Limited.

amounted to the staggering sum of £67.5 million. The repayments were to be spread over thirty-nine years at 4 per cent interest and China's maritime customs were immediately placed under foreign control for easy collection of the damages. In addition, import duties were raised and new taxes levied. With its headquarters in Shanghai, the reparation committee, comprising one delegate for each power, was empowered to receive the amount of interest and capital repayments from the Chinese authorities appointed for this task and to distribute the sums among the parties concerned. The largest proportion of the claims from the various powers went to Russia (30 per cent), Germany (20 per cent) and France (15.7 per cent). Then followed Britain with 11.2 per cent, Japan (7.7 per cent) and the United States (7 per cent), with sundry nations making up 8.4 per cent. Paradoxically, China's succession of defeats, with their disastrous economic and social effects, helped to further the development of railways, as the Chinese believed that their losses had been caused by the lack of industrialisation and technical knowledge, while at the same time hastening the revolution that was to overthrow the Manchu dynasty soon after the Empress Dowager's death. Indeed, the Imperial throne became indissolubly associated with China's repeated failures on the economic and political front.

When China entered the First World War on the Allies' side in 1917, all the members of the *Entente* except Russia agreed to have their repayments on the Boxer indemnity postponed for five years. Russia instead waived one third of her claim. With the peace treaty of Versailles at the end of the war, Germany and Austria lost all rights to their former claims. The United States had already, in 1908, abandoned half of their claim in favour of promoting the education of Chinese students in America. Later, similar agreements were entered into by all the other small creditors. But China had yet to

raise several loans well after the end of the First World War in order to finish repaying the Boxer damages.

While Britain renounced her claim altogether after the five-year moratorium, the French demanded resumption of the payments, but at the rate of exchange prevailing in 1900 instead of the post-war rate. China strongly disputed this demand and the issue was hotly debated for three years until 1925, when the 5 per cent Gold Loan (often called the Boxer Loan) was issued for the satisfaction of the Far Eastern creditors of the defunct Banque Industrielle de Chine – a semi-official French banking institution in China which had to close down in 1922, leaving many Chinese depositors without funds. The French parliament had promised that these would be protected and intended to revive the Banque with China's Boxer indemnity payments, insisting that they be made in gold. With the issue of the 1925 Gold Loan, sufficient funds were made available to the Banque for its rehabilitation. The war indemnity paid off in gold was affected to Sino-French philanthropic and educational purposes.

During the early twentieth century China applied much effort to the development of her railway system which was mainly financed by international loans. In the loan agreements concluded during that period, the foreign bankers secured not only the control over loan funds but also the management of the railway, during and after con-

Left: The 5 per cent Hukuang Railways Gold Loan was raised by the Imperial Chinese Government in 1911 and issued by a Four Power consortium of banks in Great Britain, France, Germany and the United States. This very rare £20 bond is one of a total of only 150 bonds for £20 which were issued in New York by a group of leading banks headed by J. P. Morgan & Co.

struction. Often, they also acted as purchasing agents for the supply of materials and were entitled to a commission on their cost. The Shanghai-Nanking Railway constructed at that time, was financed by the British & Chinese Corporation (a British syndicate formed by Jardine, Matheson & Co. and the Hongkong & Shanghai Banking Corporation to promote British interests in China) which was to get 20 per cent of net profits. Although the agreement stipulated a loan for £3,250,000, only £2.900,000 was issued in three instalments in 1903, 1904 and 1907. By 1911 the Chinese government wished to take a greater control in the management and administration of the railways and started to implement a policy of nationalisation. After 1906 many Chinese provincial companies had secured railway concessions mostly for patriotic reasons. If the central government found that work progressed either too slowly or unsatisfactorily, or was even suspended, it cancelled the provincial concessions and took over the direction of operations, a move which was highly unpopular with the local population. The whole country was in disarray, with internal troubles as well as conflict with foreign powers, when twelve days after the proclamation of state-ownership of trunk railways, the signing of the £6 million Hukuang Railways loan was announced on 20 May 1911. It was floated by four nations simultaneously. As a direct result of this loan agreement, a rebellion broke out in the affected provinces, already seething with agitation, and troops had to be brought into Szechuan. The revolt, which could not be contained, spread all over China. It turned into an organised revolutionary movement. In October 1911, sweeping away the Manchu throne, the revolutionary forces proclaimed a republic with a provisional government headed by Dr Sun Yat-sen.

One year later, Sun Yat-sen resigned in September 1912 in favour of Yuan Shih-kai who, faced with immense liabilities but without funds, approached the foreign banking syndicate who had issued the Hukuang loan, with a view to a major reorganisation loan. In May 1912, the consortium which originally comprised four members (Britain, France, Germany and the United States) was joined by Russia and Japan. Already before his inauguration, Yuan had come to an understanding with the group that they were to monopolise the loan. Only one month before the loan agreement was signed, the United States pulled out of the consortium under the directive of President Wilson who, upon entering office, was opposed to a particular condition of the loan which provided for the administration of the salt revenues to be placed under foreign control, like the maritime customs. The agreement for the 5 per cent Reorganisation loan for £25 million was signed – without the American bankers – on 27 April 1913. Just as the Hukuang loan had sparked off the revolution in 1911, the Reorganisation loan was met with fierce opposition mainly directed against President Yuan, accused of not having submitted the loan agreement to the recently constituted parliament prior to its signature. But, unlike the 1911 revolution, the 1913 uprisings, which were sporadic and mainly localised in the South, were easily put down.

Right: The bonds of the highest denomination in the Chinese Government 5 per cent Gold Loan of 1912, sometimes called the Crisp Loan, were those for £1000, of which a total number of 750 were issued. This loan for £10 million was raised by the Chinese government during the protracted negotiations over the 1913 Reorganisation Loan. The agreement was signed on 30 August 1912 between the Chinese Minister in London and C.Birch, Crisp & Co., a London firm of stockbrokers representing the British banking group which had arranged the finance. Due to strong opposition from the Foreign Office and from the Hongkong & Shanghai Banking Corporation defending its exclusive banking position in China, heavy pressure was brought to bear on the Chinese government to cancel the issue. Finally a compromise was reached, according to which half the loan, i.e. £5 million, was actually issued, and the rest cancelled.

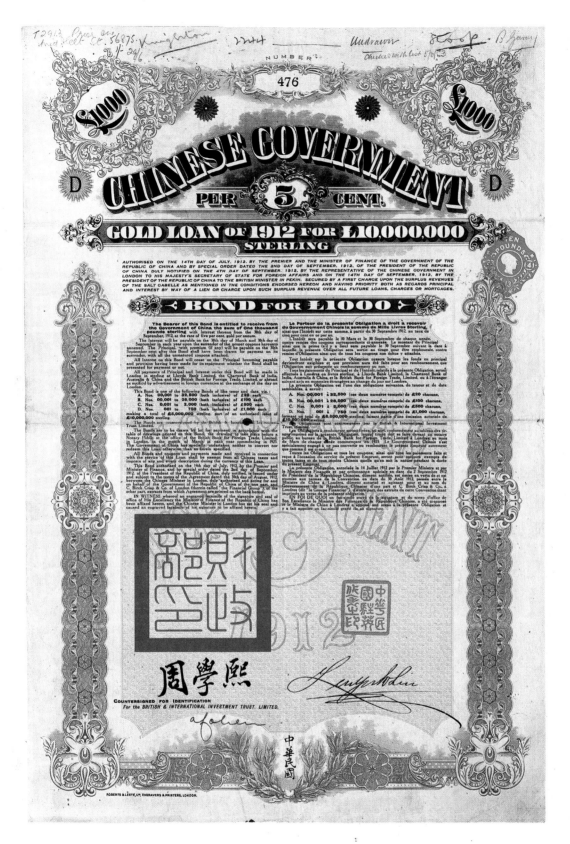

Ironically, President Wilson, who had been morally opposed to letting the United States participate in an international loan to China, himself revived the old consortium (without Germany and Russia) after the First World War with a view to floating a loan for China. This came as a counter-action against Japan's position as chief lender to China since the First World War, when none of the Western belligerents was able to float a foreign loan.

Prior to the First World War, the Chinese government, between 1912 and 1916, had raised seven loans in Austria, of which three were devoted to the purchase of naval and military armaments from the munitions factory Skoda AG, and from the Monfalcone shipbuilding yards. But due to the outbreak of the war these firms found themselves unable to complete their deliveries. Consequently China suspended repayments of the loans in 1916. After the war the Chinese Ministry of Finance, under pressure to settle its liabilities, issued a new 8 per cent loan, generally referred to as the Skoda Loan, for £6,866,046 which replaced the earlier Austrian obligations.

Post-war China was characterised by serious internal disorders, with a succession of new governments staying only a few years in power. It was not until Chiang Kai-shek established his Nationalist government in 1927 that a semblance of stability was restored. During the 1920s China's internal dissensions favoured the rise of the Kuomintang party which campaigned for the restoration of China's sovereign rights in the foreign concessions. Many of the loans issued by China during this period were for the completion of railway lines, some of which had been started by foreign companies holding concessions. The 6 per cent Indemnity Loan of 1934 for £1.5 million, secured on the British Boxer indemnity, was issued for financing the final construction of the Canton-Hankow line.

Most of China's foreign debt, of which the sterling portion amounted to some £61 million, fell into default when Japan invaded China in 1936–1937 and has not been acknowledged by the present Communist regime which came into power in 1949 when Mao Tse-tung established the People's Republic of China.

Russia

With Russian bonds, the Bolshevik revolution which swept away the Tsarist throne marks the date limit for collectors. So the Russian bonds now being collected were all issued by the same régime, the Imperial government. Similarly to China, Russia during the nineteenth century was a vast, mainly agricultural country, lagging behind its Western competitors in its industrial development, and ruled by an autocratic monarch deeply convinced of his divine right to the throne. With its feudal social institutions, Tsarist Russia was slow in attempting the reforms necessary to achieving modernisation and industrialisation on a large scale. There was strong resistance to change and innovations, from both the aristocracy and the peasant classes. Acknowledged as a more liberal ruler, Alexander II, the son of Nicholas I (who pioneered the development of steam railways in Russia), counted as his greatest achievement the emancipation of the serfs which he proclaimed in 1861. The Russian capital market

---

Left: The Chinese Government Reorganisation Loan of 1913 was raised by the Five Power consortium, composed of Britain, France, Germany, Russia and Japan. This bond for 189.40 Roubles, which forms part of the Russian tranche of the loan, is an interesting and rare variant to an otherwise ordinary bond. These brown bonds, bearing a Russian ink-stamp on the upper left-hand corner, were withdrawn and replaced by green bonds of the same denominations.

was, by and large, rudimentary and unsophisticated. Local institutions and financiers were often unable to meet the challenge of raising capital for industrial projects. For such ventures, the government had to turn to Western financial centres. With regard to Russia's railways, although part of the capital for their construction was raised on the domestic market, the bulk came from abroad.

Russian bonds issued by the Tsarist government can be divided into two categories: state funds, including bonds issued by government institutions, and bonds issued by railway companies with state guarantees. The earliest state loans quoted abroad were the 6 per cent loans of 1817 and 1818, and the 5 per cent loan of 1820. All three were listed in Amsterdam. They were raised for the redemption of assignats exactly like the 1822 state loan issued for a total of 43 million roubles, of which the portion floated abroad in sterling amounted to £6,001,030 of 38,925,600 roubles, N.M. Rothschild & Sons were the bankers handling the loan in London. A succession of other state loans issued on foreign markets followed throughout the nineteenth century. Their object was mainly to replenish or increase the Imperial Treasury, and on occasion, to convert previously issued loans. In the latter part of

the nineteenth century, a number of loans were raised to enable the state to repurchase railway lines from private companies. Such a loan was the 4 per cent Gold Loan of 1894 whose purpose was to convert the shares of the Grand Russian Railway Company, taken over by the government in 1894. Following the Treaty of Peking concluded in 1901, which settled the amount of war damages due by China to the various injured nations as a consequence of the Boxer rebellion, the Imperial Russian government, wishing to enjoy the immediate financial advantages of the reparation due by China, raised in 1902 a 4 per cent loan of 393 million marks, corresponding exactly to Russia's portion of the Boxer indemnity. Like the Chinese war reparation payments, the Russian state loan was to be redeemed over a period of thirty-nine years. Symbolising the significance of the loan, the emblems of the Russian Imperial eagle and the Chinese dragon appear on either side of the loan's title. By the late nineteenth century and during the early part of the twentieth century, an increasing number of Russian municipal loans were issued to finance improvements to city amenities.

Probably the best-known of all Russian bonds are those issued by the various railway companies. Unlike the development of railways in Britain, the United States and to a lesser extent in Europe, where private industry sought to obtain concessions for the construction and running of railways, projects for creating a railway network in Russia emanated entirely from the government, with practically no active contribution from Russian industry.

In the 1830s Nicholas I became interested in the possibilities offered by railway transport. He had received enthusiastic reports from Baron Krudener, his envoy in the United States, who had travelled in a sail-car on the Baltimore & Ohio railroad. An Austrian nobleman and engineer, Franz von Gerstner who had built many railway lines

Right: This bearer bond for 2000 German Reichsmarks forms part of the loan issued by Russia for the realisation of China's reparation of the damages suffered by Russia in consequence of the Boxer rebellion of 1900. The annual payments of the Russian State Loan were to correspond exactly with the interest and amortisation payments of the contribution China owed Russia, as defined by the Treaty of Peking of 1901. The State Loan of 1902 was issued simultaneously in Russia, Germany, Holland and Britain by a group of predominantly Russian and German banks. To symbolize the significance of the loan, the Chinese Dragon and the Russian Imperial Eagle appear on either side of the title of the bond.

ИМПЕРАТОРСКОЕ РОССІЙСКОЕ ПРАВИТЕЛЬСТВО.

РОССІЙСКІЙ
4% ГОСУДАРСТВЕННЫЙ ЗАЕМЪ 1902 г.,

выпущенный для реализаціи причитающагося Россіи отъ Китая вознагражденія на основаніи
ВЫСОЧАЙШАГО Указа 1 Марта 1902 г.

на нарицательный капиталъ въ 181.959.000 рублей,

= 393.000.000 имп. герм. марк. = 231.870.000 голл. гульд. = 19.257.000 фунт. стерл.,

въ количествѣ 22000 листовъ по 5000 имп. герм. мар. съ № 000001 по № 022000, 75000 листовъ по 2000 имп. герм. мар. съ № 022001 по № 097000, 110000 листовъ по 1000 имп. герм. мар. съ № 097001 по № 207000 и 46000 листовъ по 500 имп. герм. мар. съ № 207001 по № 253000.

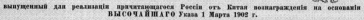

ОБЛИГАЦІЯ № 032656
ВЪ ДВѢ ТЫСЯЧИ ИМПЕРСК. ГЕРМАНСК. МАРОКЪ
= 926 руб. = 1180 голл. гульд. = 98 фунт. стерл.,

записанная въ Государственную Долговую Книгу, ин. 1, стр. 107

НА ПРЕДЪЯВИТЕЛЯ.

На основаніи ВЫСОЧАЙШАГО Указа 1 Марта 1902 года для реализаціи причитающагося Россіи вознагражденія въ возмѣщеніе убытковъ, понесенныхъ вслѣдствіе смутъ въ Китаѣ, выпускается настоящій 4% заемъ на нарицательный капиталъ въ 181.959.000 рублей, равныхъ 393.000.000 имперскимъ германскимъ маркамъ, равныхъ 231.870.000 голландскимъ гульденамъ, равныхъ 19.257.000 фунтамъ стерлинговъ, ежегодные платежи по коему находились бы въ точномъ соотвѣтствіи съ причитающимися отъ Китайскаго Правительства ежегодными уплатами процентовъ и погашенія по слѣдуемой Россіи части вознагражденія, которое Китай обязался выплатить согласно эдикту Китайскаго Императора отъ 29 Мая новаго стиля 1901 года.

Заемъ сей внесенъ въ Государственную Долговую Книгу подъ наименованіемъ „Россійскій 4% Государственный заемъ 1902 г., выпущенный для реализаціи причитающагося Россіи отъ Китая вознагражденія".

Облигаціи сего займа выпускаются именныя и на предъявителя, достоинствомъ въ 500, 1000, 2000 и 5000 имп. герм. марокъ, считая каждыя 1000 имп. герм. марокъ = 463 рублямъ = 590 голл. гульд. = 49 фунт. стерл.

Владѣлецъ сей облигаціи имѣетъ право на сумму въ ДВѢ ТЫСЯЧИ ИМПЕРСКИХЪ ГЕРМАНСКИХЪ МАРОКЪ = 926 руб., приносящую ЧЕТЫРЕ процента въ годъ дохода до погашенія оной тиражемъ или выкупомъ; теченіе процентовъ начинается съ 19 Декабря 1901 г./1 Января 1902 г.

Облигаціи сіи освобождены навсегда отъ всякихъ русскихъ налоговъ.

Проценты уплачиваются два раза въ годъ, 18 Іюня/1 Іюля и 19 Декабря/1 Января, по предъявленіи купоновъ, по желанію владѣльца:

въ РОССІИ — въ Конторахъ и Отдѣленіяхъ Государственнаго Банка — рублями;
въ ГЕРМАНІИ — имперскими германскими марками —
    — въ Берлинѣ — у гг. Мендельсонъ и К°,
      „   „   у г. С. Блейхредеръ,
      „   „   въ Дирекціи Учетнаго Общества,
      „   „   у гг. Роберъ Варшауеръ и К°,
    во Франкфуртѣ н/М., въ Дирекціи Учетн. Общества;
въ ГОЛЛАНДІИ — голландскими гульденами — у гг. Липпманъ, Розенталь и К° въ Амстердамѣ;
въ АНГЛІИ — фунтами стерлинговъ — въ Агентствѣ Русскаго для внѣшней торговли Банка въ Лондонѣ.

Облигаціи сего займа погашаются по нарицательной цѣнѣ въ теченіе 39 лѣтъ ежегодными тиражами по плану, на оборотѣ напечатанному. Тиражи будутъ производиться въ Сентябрѣ каждаго года, начиная съ 1902 г. Капиталъ по вышедшимъ въ тиражъ облигаціямъ уплачивается въ слѣдующій за тиражемъ срокъ уплаты процентовъ.

До 19 Декабря 1914/1 Января 1915 года отчисленіе на погашеніе займа не будетъ увеличиваемо сверхъ предусмотрѣннныхъ планомъ погашенія суммъ, а равно до того же срока не будетъ приступлено ни къ выкупу, ни къ конверсіи настоящаго займа.

Уплата капитала по облигаціямъ производится въ тѣхъ же городахъ и въ тѣхъ же валютахъ, какъ и уплата купоновъ, по предъявленіи самой облигаціи съ талономъ и всѣми купонами, срокъ коихъ истекаетъ послѣ срока уплаты капитала; сумма недостающихъ купоновъ будетъ удержана при выдачѣ капитала по выкупаемымъ облигаціямъ.

Облигаціи сего займа сохраняютъ платежную силу въ теченіе 30 лѣтъ со срока, назначеннаго для ихъ оплаты, а купоны сихъ облигацій — въ теченіе 10 лѣтъ со срока ихъ оплаты.

Каждая облигація сего займа снабжена купонами и талономъ для полученія новыхъ купоновъ по истеченіи старыхъ. Облигаціи сего займа выпускаются именныя и на предъявителя. Правила относительно именныхъ облигацій, ихъ перехода отъ одного лица къ другому, ихъ обмѣна на предъявительскія и обратно утверждаются Министромъ Финансовъ.

Облигаціи сего займа будутъ принимаемы по цѣнамъ, устанавливаемымъ на каждое полугодіе Министромъ Финансовъ и публикуемымъ чрезъ Правительствующій Сенатъ, въ залоги: а) по казеннымъ подрядамъ и поставкамъ, б) по разсрочиваемому акцизу и в) въ обезпеченіе таможенныхъ пошлинъ. Указанныя цѣны будутъ не ниже 90% нарицательной цѣны облигацій.

Управляющій Государственною Коммиссіею Погашенія Долговъ

Бухгалтеръ

№4055 № 4055

ЗАЕМЪ ГОРОДА НИКОЛАЕВА

на нарицательный капиталъ 6.499.899 рублей=687.820 фунтамъ стерлинговъ,

заключенный на основаніи ВЫСОЧАЙШЕ утвержденнаго 19 Сентября 1910 года положенія Совѣта Министровъ.

ОБЛИГАЦІЯ

945 РУБЛЕЙ.

ВЪ ДЕВЯТЬСОТЪ СОРОКЪ ПЯТЬ РУБЛЕЙ

=100 фунтамъ стерлинговъ

НА ПРЕДЪЯВИТЕЛЯ,

приносящая дохода 5% въ годъ,

безъ удержанія сбора съ доходовъ отъ денежныхъ капиталовъ.

LOAN OF THE CITY OF NIKOLAEF

on the nominal capital of 6.499.899 roubles=687.820 pounds sterling,

issued in virtue of a decision of the Council of Ministers, sanctioned by H. I. Majesty the EMPEROR on the 19 September 1910.

BOND

OF NINE HUNDRED AND FORTY-FIVE ROUBLES

=100 pounds sterling

TO BEARER,

bearing interest at the rate of 5% per annum,

without deduction of the tax on incomes from money funds.

Городской Голова
Mayor

Члены Управы
Members of the Municipal Administration

Бухгалтеръ
Book-keeper

Николаевъ, 1912, Nikolaef.

on the continent, approached the Tsar in 1834, with a project for a concession to build an extensive railway network in Russia. Despite strong resistance from his closest government advisers who tended to look upon railways as 'the weapon of democracy', Nicholas I, though totally opposed to any idea of social reform, nevertheless grasped the immense strategic advantages, from a military viewpoint, to be gained by railways. To begin with, he granted Gerstner a concession for a short line to run from St Petersburg to Tsarskoe Selo, the Tsar's nearby summer residence. Although it was intended as an experimental public passenger line only, it proved a great success, financially too, from the very day of its opening in 1837. Encouraged, the Tsar resolved to build the first major internal railway, linking the new capital St Petersburg with the old, Moscow. However, before the construction of this line was undertaken, Nicholas gave his consent to a concession for a line from Warsaw to Vienna which was started in 1839. Work had to be interrupted in 1841 due to insufficient funds and, eventually, the government took over the construction of the railway which was completed in 1848, just in time for the transport of Russian troops to the scene of uprisings in Hungary. In 1842, the project for the St Petersburg-Moscow line, in which the Tsar was willing to invest 34 million roubles, was announced to the public. Major George W. Whistler (the father of the famous painter), an American engineer who built a number of early railway lines in the United States, was called to Russia to supervise the construction of the line. To be 'assured of the ultimate completion of this great undertaking', Nicholas I appointed his son Alexander chairman of the railway committee. The legend says that the Tsar only once opposed Whistler on the matter of the exact path of the line. Picking up his ruler, Nicholas placed it on a map and drew a straight line, saying: 'Here is your direction'.

In fact, the St Petersburg-Moscow line is one of the straightest in the world, mainly owing to the very flat terrain, only broken up halfway by the Valdai range of mountains. Contingents of serfs and Polish captives, taken in the quelled rebellion of 1831, were brought in as labourers, thousands of whom died of scurvy, typhoid and cholera which spread alarmingly through the work camps along the line. Vodka, 'the green serpent', was deemed the best medicine and its sale encouraged by the government, no doubt because half the Treasury's income came from that particular source. The rolling-stock to be employed on the line was ordered from the United States but assembled in Russia under American supervision. The line was eventually completed in 1851 and was for a long time Russia's showpiece railway.

After the Tsar's death, his successor Alexander II renamed the line the Nicolai Railway in his father's honour. Himself a railway enthusiast, Alexander II insisted on travelling in the fastest train in the land. Because of his obsession with speed, he and his family were involved in more than one accident, as safety measures on the railway had been discarded in favour of achieving higher speeds. The South Western railway was often used by Tsar Alexander when he travelled to the Black Sea. Once the royal train, having on board the Tsar, his family and a numerous entourage, became derailed near Borki, injuring twenty-one people.

Left: This Russian loan of £687,820, bearing 5 per cent interest, was raised by the City of Nicolaef in order to purchase an already existing horse-drawn tramway owned by a Belgian company and to bring several improvements to the town's amenities. Floated in two parts, the first portion of £646,200 was offered for sale in July 1912, the second tranche of £41,620 being issued subsequently. The bond illustrated here is from the second issue, the smallest known Russian loan.

However the Imperial family were not among the victims. The derailment had been caused by a rail breaking under the excessive weight of the overloaded train, which was hauled by two heavy-goods locomotives to ensure maximum speed.

All new railway projects launched in Russia before the Crimean war were backed by a guarantee from the state, as the country showed little confidence in the profitability of the new means of transport. The high building cost of the St Petersburg-Moscow line made it evident to the government that an influx of private capital was required to develop a proper railway network in the country. After the Crimean war, a Franco-Russian consortium, backed by Pereire from the Crédit Mobilier, founded in 1856 a company entitled the Grand Russian Railway Company which had been granted concessions for the construction of an extensive railway network across Russia within ten years. From the onset, the company showed an unhappy record of mismanagement and squandering of funds. Very soon after its initaial capitalisation, several supplementary loan issues were required to keep the company afloat. In 1860 it was allowed to purchase the Nicolai railway from the government in a vain attempt to bring in a sufficient flow of income to enable it to carry out its commitments, as well as to restore confidence in its shares. Two other companies were formed around the same time as the Grand Russian Railway Company. The first, which intended to build a line from Moscow to Saratov on the Volga, enjoyed financial backing from Belgium. However, due to the dismal financial record of its rival, the Grand Russian Co., the new company, managed by the astute financier von Derviz, saw its shares fall by half, even before the subscription deadline. In an attempt to remedy the situation the company's name was altered to the Moscow-Riazan Railway Company, and for a time its plan of reaching Saratov was dropped.

As most of the company's shares were left with the underwriters, von Derviz applied to the government for permission to issue bonds in Germany. This move proved so successful that it enabled him to acquire the unsubscribed shares himself out of the profits he had made selling the bonds.

The only railway company which managed effortlessly to raise the necessary share capital was the Riga-Dvinsk Railway, backed by the Riga chamber of commerce, intent on channelling grain exports through its own port. Later, in 1863, an English company obtained a concession for a connecting line from Dvinsk to Vitebsk, and two years later, Sir Morton Peto, a British railway magnate who was always hovering between riches and bankruptcy, was granted an extremely favourable concession for the Orel-Vitebsk line, the construction of which was to facilitate Russian grain exports. The concession for the strategically vital line from Moscow to the Crimea was obtained in 1863 by a British company which also planned to build a free port in Sebastopol. During the same year, a Russian company secured another concession for a railway from Odessa to Kiev, but both companies failed to raise the necessary construction capital. In view of the line's strategic importance, the government decided to build the railway from Moscow to the Black Sea out of state funds.

Railway construction fever in Russia lasted from 1866 to 1899, reaching its peak between 1866 and 1879, followed by a lull in activities which were very pronounced again after 1891. As in the beginning, the government planned the new lines which were then concessioned out to companies. Whereas railways like the Warsaw-Vienna and the St Petersburg-Vienna lines had been built for strategic purposes, the other early Russian railways answered various commercial and economic needs. Most of these lines either radiated from Moscow, the growing industrial city, or led from the

The Grand Russian Railway Company, formed in 1857 by a Russo-French consortium, enjoyed a number of important concessions to build and operate major trunk lines in Russia. Due to the chronically shaky state of its finances, the company frequently resorted to raising additional capital through foreign loans. This bond for 625 roubles formed part of the third loan issue of 13,147,000 Roubles, bearing 3 per cent and backed by the 'absolute guarantee' of the Imperial Russian government for the payment of interest and redemption at par over seventy years. The loan was officially raised to cover the expenses of laying double tracks and augmenting the rolling and material stock. The company pledged to apply the net revenues of its St Petersburg-Warsaw and Moscow-Nijni-Novgorod lines to the interest and capital payments of the loan.

wheat-producing regions to the Baltic ports or to the Black Sea. Later, new railways were built in various industrial growth areas, meeting the demands of the sugar industry in Kiev during the 1870s and the coal-mining industry in the Donets basin during the 1880s. Finally, new strategic lines were constructed in the Caucasus and near the Caspian Sea. In the 1880s and 1890s further strategic lines were built in Central Asia and Siberia for military and colonial purposes, while the majority of other new lines contributed to the development of industrial areas. As the government attached more stringent conditions to railway concessions when railwaymania got under way at the beginning of the 1870s, the interest in Russian railway securities diminished appreciably, with shares falling below par. Even the state guarantees on bonds failed to attract investment, small investors continuing to avoid getting involved in railway finance. Only big Russian railway financiers such as Poliakov, Gubonin and von Derviz, together with banks, put up capital for railway construction. To attract a broader spectrum of investment, the Russian government then announced that it would grant its 'absolute guarantee' to railway companies in respect of interest payments. The first to benefit was the Kursk-Kiev railway, originally in state ownership, but sold to Derviz. The 5 per cent interest on the issued capital of £3 million was paid by the government from the very day of issue (instead of at commencement of construction), irrespective of the progress of work. While attracting big speculative investment, the policy of granting state guarantees on interest payments proved very expensive to the state as the railway companies tended to squander the issued capital, relying on the government to meet the obligations to the bondholders.

During the latter half of the nineteenth century, Russian railways see-sawed between private and state ownership, depending on the health of the imperial finances. During the 1860s, the government was forced to sell several of its state lines to private companies, such as the Nicolai railway and the Moscow-Kursk railway. The capital thus raised was then used to set up new state railway projects. In the 1880s the trend was reversed, with many private lines passing into government ownership, while a number of smaller railways were allowed by the government to merge or to take over adjoining lines to become more profitable. Companies thus formed include the Riazan-Ural Railway, created in 1892; the South-Eastern Railway formed in 1887 and the Moscow-Windau-Rybinsk, in 1895. By 1898 seventeen private companies still existed as against forty-four in 1886. The private companies were largely owned by banks which had raised substantial sums of capital abroad, particularly in France. At the turn of the century the Russo-Asiatic Bank was a major shareholder in the South-Eastern Railway, along with the Moscow-Kazan Railway and the Moscow-Kiev-Voronesh Railway. In 1900, with the exception of a number of secondary local lines, there were nine privately-owned railways as against twenty-two belonging to the state. One of these private lines was the Chinese Eastern Railway; two others were Polish lines. The remaining six Russian railways (Moscow-Kazan; Moscow-Kiev-Voronesh; Moscow-Windau-Rybinsk; Riazan-Ural; South Eastern and Vladikavkas) were encouraged to build new lines by the government who, until 1905, even prevented new rival companies from being formed by refusing its state guarantee. In 1900 Russia's oldest railway, the Tsarskoe Selo line, was taken over by the Moscow-Windau-Rybinsk railway, thus gaining access to St Petersburg. After 1905 railway construction in little-developed regions was firmly encouraged. By 1909 there were eleven private railway companies and by 1913 their number had increased to twenty-two.

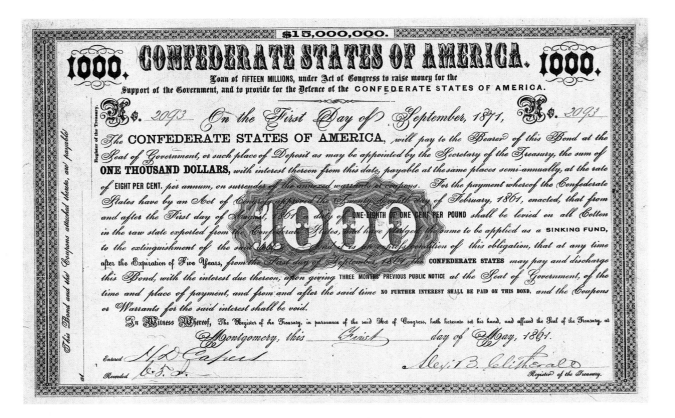

After the revolution of 1917, British holders of Russian Tsarist bonds continued for a time to receive payment of interest on their holdings. Funds to meet the coupons payable in London were provided by the British government until the end of March 1918, when it issued a statement giving notice that 'as from April 1st, 1918, holders of Russian securities must no longer look to the British Treasury for the provision of funds to meet interest due to them from Russia' and denouncing Russia's breach of international law.

The Confederate States

A famous example of violation of international law occurred when the debt contracted by the Confederate States of America was repudiated after their defeat in 1865 by the government of the United States when the 14th amendment to the constitution was passed in June 1866. This enacted that 'the United States, or any single state, shall not take over or pay any debt or liability contracted for the purpose of supporting the insurrection or rebellion against the United States'. In the winter of 1860 seven Southern states, formally seceding from the Union, proclaimed a new republic in the South, establishing a provisional government in Montgomery with Jefferson Davis as President. A United States senator, he had been a conspicuous defender of the South and of the institution of slavery, when the question of abolition which eventually led to the secession was being debated. He withdrew

97

This 'Cotton Bond', issued by the Confederate States of America on 1 June 1863 in London, and in Paris through J. Henry Schröder & Co. and Emile Erlanger & Cie respectively, formed part of a loan for £3 million, bearing 7 per cent interest and redeemable over twenty years. The interest of this rare bond lies in the stipulation that the holder had the option to convert the nominal amount of the bond into cotton, at the rate of sixpence sterling per pound of cotton.

from the Senate when the state of Mississippi seceded. In 1861 four other states joined the seven rebels.

The split from the United States, which occurred suddenly, was the result of a long-drawn-out conflict over the projected emancipation of the slaves in the Southern states. While slavery had long since been abolished in the North, it was nevertheless still recognised in fifteen states. The issue came to a head in 1860, when the Democratic party, divided over the question of slavery, lost the presidential elections to the minority Republican party. Their newly-elected president, Abraham Lincoln, was a confirmed abolitionist and it naturally followed that the Southern states believed that he would immediately enforce the unconditional emancipation of negro slaves. The diametrically opposed views between the Northern and Southern states heightened other differences between the two. The whole structure of economic life in the South was based on agriculture, while Northern states were highly industrialised. Whereas the cotton and tobacco planters in the South advocated free trade, the manufacturers in the North, battling against foreign competition, loudly demanded protectionist measures and tariff barriers against foreign products. Political opinion in the South was convinced that the Northern states would forcibly impose on the South the principle of emancipation of slaves by depriving it of its charter of liberty. As the states composing the Union were each semi-autonomous entities responsible for their own system of raising taxes, administering justice and enforcing law and order, the states in favour of slavery considered the abolition demands of the North as unconstitutional interference in domestic affairs.

The outbreak of open hostilities was therefore unavoidable. The immediate aims of the new state were two-fold: they needed both political recognition abroad and financial aid to sustain the costly war effort. The

Confederacy was given a permanent constitution in March 1861. Within four months, although failing to obtain diplomatic recognition as an independent state, the Confederates were nevertheless considered as belligerents by Britain, France and by the Congress of the United States, and as such they were entitled to international rights.

Proceeding to raise funds, the Confederacy issued its own currency and floated internal as well as external bonds. The internal bonds issued in dollars were meant for national circulation but a large number of them found their way abroad. The Confederate government also sought to raise finance directly on foreign markets. For this purpose, it issued in 1863 the 7 per cent Cotton Loan for £3 million in Europe through J. Henry Schröder & Co. in London, and Emile Erlanger et Cie in Paris. A special provision of the agreement stipulated that the bondholder was given the option of having the loan either redeemed in cash or converted into the equivalent amount of cotton delivered to him at the rate of 6d. per pound. These bonds were primarily destined for the British who had a strong interest in the survival of the cotton-producing states on which a large portion of their manufacturing industry was heavily dependent for its prosperity. During the course of the war, the South redeemed some £800,000 of bonds against cotton, while duly paying interest on the balance. When the Confederates were eventually defeated in 1865, the cotton allocated for the repayment of the loan was seized by the Unionists and either sold or burnt. The naval blockade imposed by the Federal navy, although seriously hindering shipments of cotton vital to the Lancashire mills, was, however, frequently broken. English shipowners, at great risk to themselves, established a steady flow of trade between the South and the continent, sending munitions and medicines in exchange for cotton and tobacco. For this purpose, the Bahamas and Bermuda were used as bases for the storage of goods.

With the initial military victories of the Confederacy, Wall Street stocks fell in New York while the price of gold rose sharply. In December 1862, after General Lee's victory at Fredericksburg on the 13th, President Jefferson Davis confidently expected the war to be soon over, and the Confederacy recognised in its own right by the major European powers. The following year began auspiciously for the South with the Federal army being beaten again at Chancellorsville in May 1863, and General Lee advancing with his troops into Pennsylvania. However, the tide of war turned against the South with the Confederates' decisive defeat at Gettysburg in July 1863. Vastly superior in number and equipment, the Northern armies continued wearing down the Southern forces. Finally, the Confederate armies, in the person of General Lee, formally surrendered in Richmond after a long and particularly harsh siege.

After the capitulation, the re-entry of the Southern states into the Union became conditional on their repudiation of any liability for loans that were contracted during the war, in accordance with the new amendment of the United States constitution ratified in June 1866.

In London, a committee of principal Confederate bondholders was formed in 1883 when the Southern states were recovering from the ravages of the war, with the intention of defending their claim on repayment of the defaulted loans. At this stage, British bondholders were invited to hand in their certificates to the committee's trustees in exchange for scrip certificates of deposit issued by the National Safe Deposit Company which arranged for safe custody of the bonds.

As late as 1924 British holders of Confederate bonds still upheld the liability of the Southern states for their war debts, while exonerating the United States government.

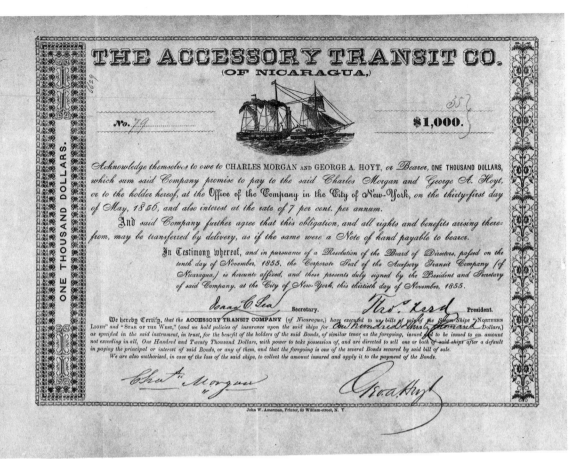

THE ACCESSORY TRANSIT CO.
(OF NICARAGUA,)

No. 79

$1,000.

Acknowledge themselves to owe to CHARLES MORGAN AND GEORGE A. HOYT, *or Bearer,* ONE THOUSAND DOLLARS, *which sum said Company promise to pay to the said Charles Morgan and George A. Hoyt, or to the holder hereof, at the Office of the Company in the City of New-York, on the thirty-first day of May, 1856, and also interest at the rate of 7 per cent. per annum.*

And said Company further agree that this obligation, and all rights and benefits arising therefrom, may be transferred by delivery, as if the same were a Note of hand payable to bearer.

In Testimony whereof, and in pursuance of a Resolution of the Board of Directors, passed on the tenth day of November, 1855, the Corporate Seal of the Accessory Transit Company (of Nicaragua,) is hereunto affixed, and these presents duly signed by the President and Secretary of said Company, at the City of New-York, this thirtieth day of November, 1855.

Isaac C. Sea Secretary.   *Thos. Lord* President.

We hereby Certify, *that the* ACCESSORY TRANSIT COMPANY *(of Nicaragua,) have executed to us bills of sale of the Steam-Ships "*NORTHERN LIGHT*" and "*STAR OF THE WEST,*" (and we hold policies of insurance upon the said ships for One Hundred and Thirty Thousand Dollars,) as specified in the said instrument, in trust, for the benefit of the holders of the said Bonds, of similar tenor as the foregoing, issued and to be issued to an amount not exceeding in all, One Hundred and Twenty Thousand Dollars, with power to take possession of, and are directed to sell one or both of said ships after a default in paying the principal or interest of said Bonds, or any of them, and that the foregoing is one of the several Bonds secured by said bill of sale.*

We are also authorized, in case of the loss of the said ships, to collect the amount insured and apply it to the payment of the Bonds.*

Chas. Morgan   *Geo. A. Hoyt*

John W. Amerman, Printer, 60 William-street, N. Y.

ONE THOUSAND DOLLARS.

The Accessory Transit Company was formed in 1850 by Commodore Cornelius Vanderbilt to provide an overland transport service across Nicaragua, on the New York to California sea route. In 1953, Cornelius Vanderbilt, about to embark on a protracted tour round Europe, resigned the presidency in favour of Charles Morgan who, in a number of complicated speculations and manipulations with the company's affairs, succeeded in gaining total control, to the other stockholders' detriment, and in making over to himself personally the company's privileges by altering its charter. An example of these machinations, this $1000 bond, dated 30 November 1855 and maturing on 31 may 1856, established Charles Morgan in partnership with George Hoyt, as creditor of the company.

7 Bonds and Shares with an outstanding History

From the vast legions of British and foreign stock companies that were created in every imaginable sector of trade and industry, this chapter will attempt to describe the early history of a mere handful, selected either because they pioneered in a new field, developed into well-established and world-famous institutions, or were formed for some eccentric reason. Included in this latter category is the story of one of the most phenomenal hoaxes ever made, that of the loan successfully raised on behalf of the non-existent state of Poyais. The companies mentioned in the following pages by chance happen to be either British or American. This has no special relevance, other than the fact that the industrial revolution, which first took place in Britain, was to have a deep and lasting effect on the development of the United States, transforming an emerging nation into a world power whose economic strength still reigns supreme. It will be noted also that the railway and transport sector has been given a predominant place. Though railways have nowadays lost much of their former importance, they represented in the nineteenth century the essential ingredient for a country's economic and industrial success.

The Baltimore and Ohio Railroad Company

With the Baltimore and Ohio Railroad Company, we enter into the pioneering age of railway development in the United States. Fearing a decline in trade as a result of the completion of the Erie Canal which tended to attract business to Philadelphia and New York, Baltimore industrialists in the second decade of the nineteenth century conceived the idea of connecting the navigable waters of the Chesapeake Bay with those of the Ohio River by means of a railway to protect their business interests.

In February 1827, the State of Maryland granted a charter of incorporation to a joint-stock company entitled 'The Baltimore & Ohio Railroad Company', to construct a railway from the city of Baltimore to the Ohio River. Its share capital of £5 million was initially three times oversubscribed, with 22.000 citizens in Baltimore alone applying for the stock. On 4 July 1828, 'Independence Day', a jubilant celebration at which the whole town was present marked the commencement of work on the line. After the opening of the first section, three miles in length, laid during 1828–1829, the favourite method of conveyance on the rails was a flat, open horsedrawn carriage in which passengers had to stand as there were no seats. Other experiments, including 'sail-cars', were also tried.

By spring 1830, 14 miles of track were completed and the Baltimore & Ohio Railroad attracted quite a lot of attention as it was, in its project to link the Atlantic to the Mississippi Valley, America's first long distance line. With the advertisements of the

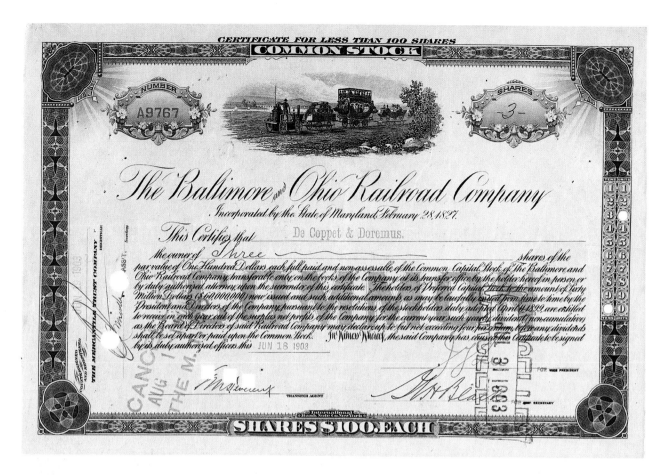

This attractive share certificate in the Baltimore & Ohio Railroad Company,
first incorporated in 1827, was issued in 1903 after the company's
reconstruction of 1899. The vignette, reminiscent of the railway's pioneering
days, depicts the engine 'Tom Thumb', the first steam locomotive built in the
United States, on its trial run in 1830.

company's daily rail services in the Baltimore *American,* the first railway timetable
appeared in the United States. During that
time, the Russian Tsar's envoy in America,
Baron Krudener, also had a ride on the Baltimore & Ohio, in the sail-car 'Aeolus',
which having steered it himself he declared
to be a most exhilarating means of transport.

However, the company had also been considering the introduction of steam engines on
the railway, although existing restricting
regulations specifically prohibited steam-propelled trains to enter the city of Baltimore itself. A further handicap was the
prevailing technical opinion, both in the
United States and Europe, which held it
impossible to use steam engines on the Baltimore & Ohio track as constructed, because
of the steepness of the curves and gradients.
Meanwhile, a local Baltimore landowner,
Peter Cooper, gluemaker by profession and

amateur inventor in his spare time, was convinced that steam would prove the key factor to the eventual success and prosperity of both the railway and the city. On 28 August 1830, he put on the track of the Baltimore & Ohio, America's first steam locomotive, an experimental engine that he had built himself. On this trial run, Peter Cooper's 'Tom Thumb' moved off with the first load of passengers ever driven by steam in the country. It ran the whole distance of approximately 14 miles without a break in one and a quarter hours, and achieved the even faster time of 57 minutes on the way back, during which it competed with a horse-driven carriage in an improvised race, in the end won by the horse, after the engine suffered a sudden loss of steam when a rope gearing fell out of place. Nevertheless, it had been an undisputed victory in favour of steam: the 'Tom Thumb', crude and unsophisticated as it was, proved without a

This beautiful $1000 bond, with sterling conversion at £200, was issued by the Blue Ridge Railroad on 1 July 1869 and guaranteed by the State of South Carolina under the Act of 1868. The projected scheme was to extend the short line that already existed from Anderson to Walhalla in order to connect Charleston in South Carolina to Knoxville in Tennessee. By virtue of an Act passed no later than 1872, the State, in order to relieve itself of all liability for its guarantee on the bonds, issued special 'revenue bond scrips' for securing and subsequently destroying the same bonds which were declared null and void.

shadow of a doubt that steam transport on the Baltimore & Ohio was a feasibility. Already in 1831, of the five American engine designs submitted, the company selected Phineas Davis's 'York', a four-wheeled engine with vertical boiler which became the pioneer engine in regular service on the railway.

Meanwhile the construction of the line progressed westwards, although hampered at first by fierce opposition from turnpike and canal companies. In August 1835, a train with seventeen coaches pulled into Washington, the federal capital, which obtained its first rail connection. Soon after this event, the federal government recommended that mail between Baltimore and Washington should be carried by rail rather than by mail-coach. The country's first mail wagons were introduced on the Baltimore & Ohio shortly afterwards.

In 1837 the railway extended as far as the Cumberland Gap, beyond which lay a difficult mountainous section, but the company's resources were exhausted. So that the line could be completed as far as the Ohio River, the company had received from the State of Maryland and the city of Baltimore an additional loan of $3 million each, on which it had to pay 6 per cent interest. In that year's difficult economic conditions, following a very harsh winter during which passenger traffic had declined by 20 per cent, the company's newly issued bonds, guaranteed both by the state and the city, could not even be sold at a discount, as the public had no money to invest and the banks were reluctant to advance the capital. Faced with an acute shortage of funds, the desperate directors resorted to paying railway contractors in these unsaleable bonds and their labourers in scrip to be later redeemed in goods or cash in Baltimore. Eventually, Baring Brothers, the London merchant bankers, came to the rescue and took the railway bonds in 1848. This helped to finance the line's most expensive section through the

Cumberland mountains. The railway actually reached the Ohio River at Wheeling, Virginia, in 1852.

From the late 1840s onward, American railway development benefited increasingly from the influx of foreign capital. Much later, during the American Civil War, the Southern States were able to rely on a certain amount of financial help from abroad precisely because of these early investments – many of them British –, in Southern enterprises, as foreign investors calculated that they ran greater risks of losing their holdings in the South if the Confederacy suffered a defeat, as the North would hardly recognise former pledges.

The American Express Company

Today the American Express Company has become a household name all over the world for its banking, travelling and credit services. Its Travellers Cheques and little green and white plastic credit cards, widely used by millions of people, are synonymous with safety and reliability, two qualities the company wanted to be associated with when it was first created in 1850 by the now legendary figures of Henry Wells and William G. Fargo, together with five other business partners. The company's activities were then of quite a different nature. In those days, private companies used to engage in the business of conveying goods, valuables and money safely and swiftly to their destination, as there was yet no established parcel post service in the United States. With the country's fast industrial growth and the opening-up of new territories in the West by means of numerous railway lines being eagerly built, these 'express' companies were doing a thriving and lucrative business, satisfying an urgent social need.

The express business had been flourishing for about fifteen years when, on 18 March 1850, Henry Wells, head of Wells & Co.,

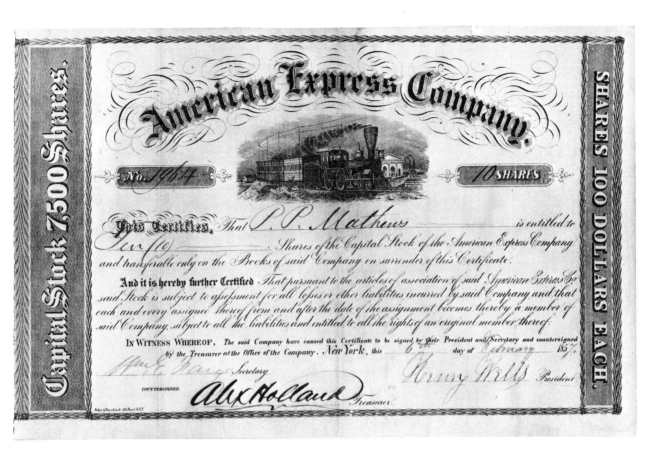

This early share in the capital stock of the American Express Company was issued on 6 February 1857. The company was created in 1850 by Henry Wells and William Fargo whose signatures in ink appear at the bottom of the certificate. An unincorporated association, it was capitalised at a mere $150,000, with each shareholder personally liable for the company's losses.

suggested a meeting between the partners of his two major competitors, Livingston & Fargo & Co., and Butterfield & Wasson. The outcome was that the three companies sold all their express lines and business to a newly-formed entity, the 'American Express Company', of which virtually all the former partners became directors. An unincorporated association, it was capitalised at a modest $150,000 with Henry Wells elected president. The owners of the compa-

ny's shares stood personally liable for all its debts. A special provision of the articles of association stipulated that the shares could not be bought without approval of the board of directors or be sold to 'married women, infants or irresponsible persons'.

Very early on, it became apparent to express companies that special contracts with the various railways were essential to ensure the fast forwarding of goods. Henry Wells' in his early career as an express messenger, used to carry goods and valuables in a large carpetbag for which he bought a ticket for an extra seat on the train. He was among the first to see the need for negotiating a flat commutation rate with railway companies. American Express forged close links with the New York and Erie Railway, later the New York Central Railway.

In 1852, Wells and his vice-president, William Fargo, proposed to extend the company's operations to the far west to handle the lucrative express trade that originated from the Californian gold mines. The gold was mostly shipped east by sea route, via the Isthmus of Panama. As the other directors were opposed to the idea, Wells and Fargo instigated a venture of their own, named 'Wells, Fargo & Co.' – later to become a leading enterprise in the west. It maintained a close working agreement with the American Express Co., whereby the express business west of the Missouri River was handled by Wells, Fargo & Co., the American Express Co. itself operating to the east of it. A few years later, another founder-director, John Butterfield, launched a new venture: the Overland Mail, by the famous pony express, which covered the distance from Chicago to San Francisco. Within ten years of its formation, the American Express Co. had become the country's foremost express carrier when, in accordance with its articles of association, its span of life ran out. The shareholders were advised that the company was to be dissolved and its assets sold at a public auction. A meeting was convened in order to form a new company which would bid in the old. Thus, the old company disappeared, giving way to the new American Express Co., purchased by the shareholders for $600,000.

One of the first new challenges it had to face was the Civil War. There was no shortage of business: the American Express was fully occupied transporting vital supplies to army depots on behalf of the Federal government and advancing in the wake of the triumphant Northern armies, delivering parcels to the overrun parts of the Confederacy through its expressmen enlisted in the Union's forces. After the war, as business generally declined, the American Express Co. had to face serious, and in one case damaging, competition. Its most dangerous rival was the Merchants Union Express Company, with which it engaged in a bitter price war between 1867 and 1868, with both parties suffering heavy losses. In the end, the two companies merged in 1868 under the name 'the American Merchants Union Express Company'.

Affected by the strain of the conflict, Henry Wells resigned from the presidency in 1868 shortly before the merger. His old partner William Fargo succeeded him as president, first of the American Merchants Union Express Co., then as from 1873, of the American Express Co. when the 'Merchants Union' was dropped from its name, until his death in 1881. Under the presidency of William Fargo's younger brother James Congdell Fargo, who for the next thirty-five years autocratically controlled the company's destiny, the American Express Co. expanded and diversified its activities. J.C. Fargo himself was directly responsible for two innovations, the introduction of the American Express Money Order in 1882 – as a challenge to the United States postal money order – and the 'Travellers Cheque' in 1891, following his own difficulties in obtaining cash with the usual letters of credit during his European tour. However, J.C. Fargo categorically and steadfastly refused to allow the company to enter into the travel business proper. He was equally adamant about employing women, as can be judged from his letter to the manager of the Paris office: 'When the day comes that American Express has to hire a female employee, it will close its doors!' The first foreign office was opened in Paris in 1891 to handle freight and was soon followed by others in the major European ports. Despite J.C. Fargo's strict decree regarding tourism, the scope of their activities soon extended towards the travel business. Indeed, with his resignation in 1914 and the outbreak of the First World War, a whole era came to an end.

No later than 1915, a proper Travel Department was created. A severe blow for the company came in December 1917, when the United States government announced that it was taking over all the country's railways to co-ordinate the war effort. Thus, the hard-won contracts between railways and express companies were abruptly terminated. This was soon followed by another decision, even more dramatic and final. In the interest of efficiency, the government amalgamated all existing express companies into one single giant concern. All the companies sold their equipment and received in return shares in the new company, the American Railway Co. Inc., which came into being on 1 July 1918. For the American Express Co., this meant that, after more than half a century of engaging in the express trade, the reason for its existence and the backbone of its earnings had vanished. Instead, the company concentrated on its already flourishing and profitable sidelines, like the financial and banking services in the form of travellers cheques, money orders, foreign remittances and foreign exchange, the international freight forwarding business and the fast-developing travel department. These activities still form the core of the company's business today.

The Merchants Union Express Company

The Merchants Union Express Company, whose history is closely linked to the American Express Co., dates back to the pioneering days when the United States, having just emerged from the trauma of a civil war, were occupied in rebuilding their economy and experiencing a veritable railway boom amidst great industrial development. In the absence of a government parcel-post service, private companies engaged in fierce competition to secure express business. It was quite a profitable operation, especially when the company involved feared practically no competition on its service routes and could negotiate exclusive freight contracts with the railways.

This was the situation in 1867, when a large group of merchants from the state of New York, disgruntled about the high rates charged by established companies, decided to join their efforts and form their own express company entitled 'The Merchants Union Express Company, and highly capitalised at $20 million. Immediately after its successful launching, it became locked in a ruthless price war with its nearest rival, the American Express Co. The two fought a merciless battle, undercutting their rates, enticing each other's men away and resorting to any means at their disposal to increase their volume of business.

The fight lasted over a year, both parties inflicting on each other serious losses. Whereas before, the American Express Co. used to earn practically $100,000 a month, it was forced to suspend dividend payments during 1867 because its losses reached $250,000 per month. The situation was hardly any better for the Merchants Union. After one year of operation, it had lost $7 million. On the brink of financial collapse, the two called for a truce and agreed on a merger in order to survive. In 1868, the Merchants Union Express Co. amalgamated with the American Express Co. to become the American Merchants Union Express Co., capitalised at $18 million, to which each party contributed equally. The new board of directors was composed of the same men who had previously been bitter

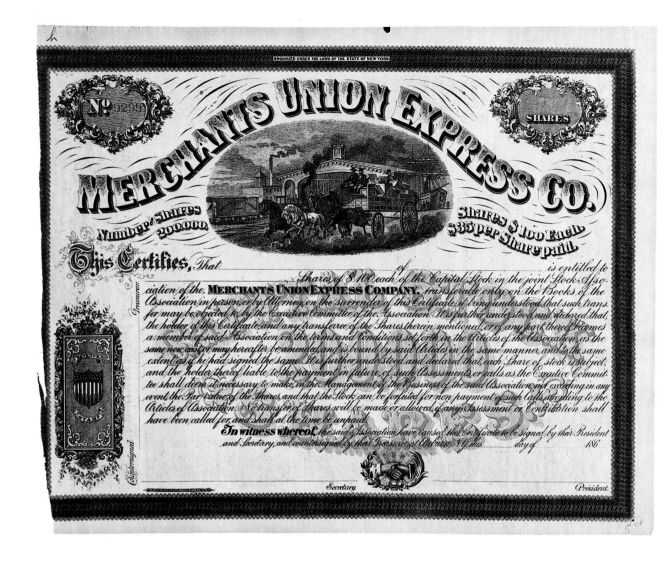

This unissued share certificate belongs to the Merchants Union Express
Company, incorporated in the state of New York in 1867 and famous for its
ruthless price war against its main rival, the American Express Company, with
which it amalgamated in 1868 under the name of 'The American Merchants
Union Express Company'.

enemies. The name 'Merchants Union' survived until 1873, when the American
Express Co. purchased the rights to drop
it from its title.

The Strand Bridge Company

While John Stow, in his *Survey of the Cities
of London and Westminster* in 1720 applied
the term 'Strand Bridge' to a bridge in the
Strand that used to carry the roadway over
a brook (where Catherine Street now runs),
at the beginning of the nineteenth century,
it referred to the work of John Rennie, a

strikingly elegant piece of civil architecture on the Thames which had been financed by a joint-stock company.

The Strand Bridge Company was incorporated in 1809 by an Act of Parliament, which authorised it to raise £500,000 in shares of £100 each, with the provision of another £300,000 by new shares or mortgage if necessary, for the purpose of erecting a bridge over the Thames, near the Strand. In July 1813, a second Act of Parliament enabled the company to raise a further sum of £200,000. Finally, a third Act passed in 1816 allowed for the name of the bridge to be changed into 'Waterloo Bridge', in honour of the great battle that had recently been won. The victory over Napoleon had so captured the imagination of the public that the names 'Wellington' and 'Waterloo' were freely used to refer to a number of things, ranging from streets to boots, and hotels to bonnets!

The light and elegant design of the bridge, of which Canova, the famous artist, declared it was 'the noblest bridge in the world, alone worth coming from Rome to London to see', consisted of nine semi-elliptical arches – with Doric columns adorning the front of the piers – covered by a cornice, and surmounted by a balustrade. The first stone was laid on 11 October 1811. While the bridge was still under construction in 1814, Tsar Alexander I, on a visit to London, exclaimed on one of his frequent inspections of the works that it would be the finest work of masonry in the world.

This share certificate printed on parchment paper and dated 30 December 1809 was issued by the Strand Bridge Company, incorporated by Act of Parliament in 1809 for the purpose of building the said bridge. The original capital was £500,000, divided into shares of £100. In 1816, the name of the bridge was changed to the 'Waterloo Bridge', in honour of the battle recently won.

The ceremony of inaugurating the bridge was performed by the Prince Regent on the second anniversary of the battle of Waterloo, 18 June 1817. It was a glittering occasion, attended by royalty, the Duke of Wellington himself and a brilliant staff of officers who had served at the historic battle. As an investment however, the new Waterloo Bridge was far from profitable for the shareholders in the Strand Bridge Company. The cost alone of building the bridge and its approaches was estimated to have reached roughly £1 million. Although tolls were levied (one halfpenny for foot passengers, twopence for cabs, etc.), the income derived from them never attained the level of the construction costs. From the first opening of the bridge until 1873, when the question of abolishing tolls was being debated, the company had collected a total of £851,760 in tolls. The income from tolls amounted to £21,000 per annum in the years just preceding the elimination of toll levies. The present-day Waterloo Bridge is a recent construction, erected by Sir Giles G. Scott in 1945.

The Stockton and Darlington Railway Company

In Great Britain, the growing demands of commerce had led, in the early nineteenth century, to a general discontent with the existing means of communications. Dr James Anderson, in his book entitled *Recreations in Agriculture,* advocated as early as 1800, the construction of railways alongside turnpike roads for a more efficient transport of heavy loads as well as passengers. However, tramroads, though already in use in mines, were still isolated undertakings. Heavy freight was largely moved on canals which enjoyed a quasi-monopoly, their owners therefore able to charge high rates. Dissatisfaction with the system was particularly strong in South

Durham, a region rich in coal but remote from sea ports. The construction of a canal, though envisaged at first, was eventually dropped in favour of that of a tramway with wooden rails, on which wagons would be drawn by horses or by ropes attached to stationary engines. After George Stephenson's appointment as engineer and surveyor of the projected line, the wooden rail scheme was replaced by one using iron rails and the idea of a steam locomotive to provide haulage was adopted.

By the end of 1816, steps had been taken towards forming a company for the purpose of building the intended railway. After three unsuccessful applications, the company was incorporated by Parliament on 19 April 1821 under the name of the 'Stockton & Darlington Railway Company'. Ironically, strong opposition had come precisely from Stockton business circles, including coalmine owners, who stood to gain most from the railway. In 1818, the scheme had been vetoed by Lord Darlington because the projected line threatened to run through one of his fox coverts. His antagonism intensified upon receiving the news, while he was out hunting, that he was summoned to London for a debate on the project.

The bulk of the share capital in the company was recruited through the personal capital market of the Quakers, under the driving force and initiative of a leading Darlington Quaker, Edward Pease who was the line's most fervent advocate. Because of the Quakers' financial involvement, the railway used to be called 'the Quakers' line' by contemporaries.

Started in 1822, construction lasted until 1825, by which time the company had used up all of its authorised capital and borrowings. Nevertheless, despite initial difficulties the railway very rapidly became a financial success. The official opening of the line was fixed on 27 September 1825. 'Locomotion no. 1', the six-ton steam engine designed and, on the inaugural day, driven by George

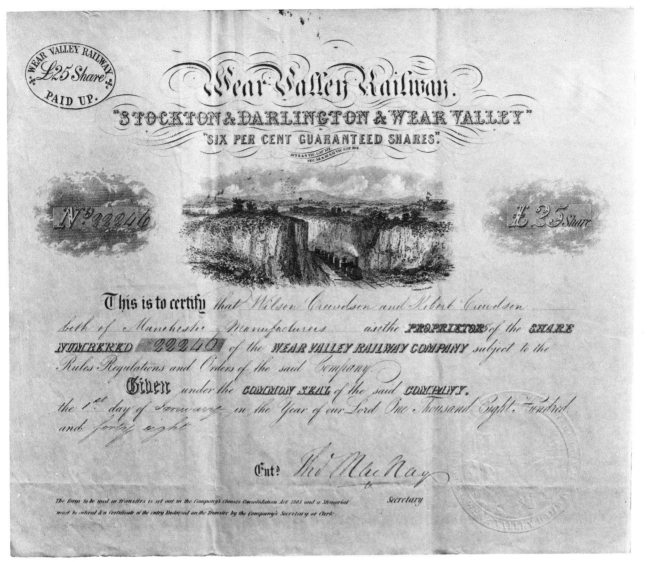

Wear Valley Railway.

"STOCKTON & DARLINGTON & WEAR VALLEY"

"SIX PER CENT GUARANTEED SHARES".

Nº 22246

£25 Share

This is to certify that *Wilson Crewdson and Robert Crewdson* both *of Manchester Manufacturers* as the PROPRIETORS of the SHARE NUMBERED *22246* of the WEAR VALLEY RAILWAY COMPANY subject to the *Rules Regulations and Orders of the said Company.* Given under the COMMON SEAL of the said COMPANY. the *1st* day of *January* in the Year of our Lord One Thousand Eight Hundred and *forty eight.*

Ent? *Thos MacNay*

Secretary

The form to be used in Transfers is set out in the Company's Clauses Consolidation Act 1845 and a Memorial must be entered & a Certificate of the entry Endorsed on the Transfer by the Company's Secretary or Clerk.

Stephenson, pulled a long train of thirty-eight wagons mainly laden with coal – although several of them also transported passengers – all the way from Stockton to Darlington, at an average speed of about eight miles per hour. As a direct result of the railway's construction, the coal trade in South Durham developed enormously, with coal prices becoming very competitive. Large export orders soon followed. Even before 1830, shares in the Stockton & Darlington Railway stood at a premium, with plenty of buyers but no sellers. Able to distribute 5 per cent dividends to its share-

This £25 bearer share was issued in 1848 by the Wear Valley Railway which was first leased to, then taken over by, the Stockton & Darlington Railway. The latter in its turn amalgamated with the North Eastern Railway Company in 1863. Thomas MacNay, whose signature appears at the bottom of the certificate, remained secretary to the Stockton & Darlington Railway Co. until and beyond the 1863 merger.

This share certificate was issued in 1868 by the Dundee, Perth and London Shipping Company, incorporated in 1826 by contract of co-partnery. It used to operate a regular passenger and freight service between London and the ports on the Tay, first by sailing vessels, then by paddle-steamers. Thomas Couper, whose signature appears on the certificate, was the company's manager from 1844 until 1879. In his years of service he witnessed the change from paddle to screw steamers which were introduced in 1856, while sailing ships, mainly trading to the Baltic, remained in operation until 1863 when the last schooner was disposed of. Still in existence today, although under a slightly altered name, the company now operates a containerised rail freight service.

holders after only the second year of trading, the company paid in 1837 and 1838 14 per cent dividends which were increased to 15 per cent from 1839 till 1841. The Stockton & Darlington was then the railway offering the highest return on capital in Britain.

The company, which at times employed management methods more suited to a private than a public enterprise, used to plough back profits into new capital expenditure and re-invest dividends for building branch-

lines and extensions. The original Act of 1821 had authorised, as another means of raising capital, the issue of promissory notes exchangeable for shares; however, as from 1828, any further note issue was prohibited partly as a result of the recent introduction of joint-stock banking, sanctioned by Parliament in 1826. In the late 1830s and during the 1840s, additional capital was obtained through the unorthodox method of retaining a portion of the dividends as a loan. In place of the retained dividends, the company would issue to its shareholders bonds bearing 5 per cent interest, with option of conversion into shares. Much earlier, at a time when the company's finances had been less secure, it had had to rely on loans from a director, after a poor response to an advertisement for share subscription. In the 1850s, however, dividends soared as high as 20 per cent.

In addition to its branch lines, the company also leased a number of neighbouring railways which were eventually taken over. The Wear Valley Railway, incorporated in 1845, was leased to the Stockton & Darlington Railway in 1847. By the Act of 23 July 1858, the Stockton & Darlington Railway was authorised to amalgamate with four other railway companies, previously leased (one of which being the Wear Valley Railway), as well as to increase its share capital to construct new lines interconnecting with the various railway systems, while retaining its original name. But eventually, the Stockton & Darlington Railway, in its turn, merged on 13 July 1863 with the North Eastern Railway. Its shares remained as a separate issue until 1869, while the company maintained in its own hands the management of its system even longer, until 1873.

The Poyais Loan of 1823

According to Gregor MacGregor I, 'Prince of Poyais and Cazique of the Poyer Nation',

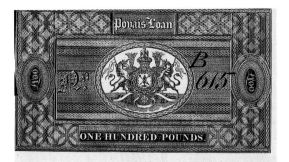

The £200,000 loan for the service of the fictitious 'State and Government of Poyais' was issued in bearer bonds of £100 each on 6 October 1823 by the bankers Sir John Perring & Co. in London. Each bond, carrying the test of the loan agreement entered into by Gregor MacGregor, Prince of Poyais, was personally signed and sealed by his associate, Major William Richardson, in his capacity as Chargé d'Affaires. (Detail)

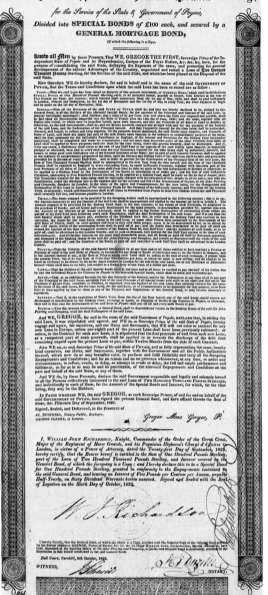

Poyais was no less than paradise on earth, a little-known but extremely rich and fertile country somewhere in Central America, blessed with a democratic form of government and proud of its large and modern capital, located at the mouth of the Black River on the Atlantic shore. This was the propaganda that MacGregor I spread in London, on his visit to raise a loan of £200,000 through the bankers Sir John Perring & Co., of Cornhill, on 15 September 1823, 'for the purpose of consolidating the said State, defraying the expenses of the same and promoting the general development of the natural advantages of the country'. The loan was divided into 'special bonds' of £100, each witnessed by the Poyaisian Chargé d'Affaires in London, William John Richardson, Knight and Commander of the Order of the Green Cross.

The reality of this supposed land of milk and honey was however very different. The whole state of Poyais, with its administration, industry, agriculture, gold and silver mines, and modern settlements, only existed in the fertile imagination of the self-styled Prince of Poyais, Gregor Mac-Gregor I. The intrepid Scotsman, descended from an old Highland family, was looking for fresh fields of activity when he landed in 1820 with a small army of soldiers on a swampy and desolate part of the Atlantic coast of Nicaragua, called the Mosquito Shore because of the Mosquito Indians that inhabited it, after having successfully fought at the side of Simon Bolivar in the Venezuelan wars of liberation, during which he had won the rank of general. Finding this inhospitable land only sparsely occupied by tribes of Indians. MacGregor easily persuaded the chief of the Poyais Indians who lived in the interior to grant him a concession for the territories along the coast against the promise of many riches to come with colonisation and settlement. Having conferred on his person suitably impressive titles of his own fabrication, MacGregor returned to England with his entourage, including Richardson, an old comrade in arms from the Venezuelan wars, whom he had decorated with the invented Order of the Green Cross.

The scheme he intended to pursue was to attract settlers to his country of Poyais, hoping that through their own work they would turn his promises into reality. For this purpose, immigration offices were set up soon after his arrival in England, plots of land were sold at four shillings an acre and arrangements to raise the notorious state loan were made. Received at Court, MacGregor was knighted by George III for his work in establishing good relations between the two countries! Prospective immigrants desperately looking for a brighter future, as well as financial circles eager to invest in some new lucrative venture, were all the more easily duped as knowledge and accurate information about Central America were lacking.

Towards the end of 1822, the first immigration ship, the *Honduras Packet* sailed for Poyais with some two hundred settlers on board. Altogether, no fewer than seven ships sailed to the non-existent state. When they arrived, instead of setting eyes on the beautiful capital with its well-appointed port, they found nothing but a deserted swampland infested with diseases. The few angry survivors who managed to return to England trickled back from the autumn of 1824 onwards, to relate their sorry tale.

In the meantime, MacGregor, accompanied by his suite, had left England for Paris where he also succeeded in forming a number of companies to develop Poyais. In 1825 the first group of French settlers sailed from Le Havre. Even by that time, the news of the real state of affairs had not yet managed to penetrate the City of London, as a further loan of £300,000 was floated by bankers Thomas Jenkins & Co., against the security of the imaginary Paulaza gold mines. By 1827 however, when MacGregor returned to London, thinking that the immediate danger of being discovered was over, the story of Poyais was only too well-known and he was arrested immediately on arrival. But soon after, thanks to influential people in high places who had been involved in so successfully arranging the Poyais loan, and who feared a scandal in which their names would be mentioned, MacGregor was released from jail and hastily retreated to Paris where, to his dismay, a similar scene was enacted. It was the end of the great Poyais myth, despite MacGregor's attempt at another comeback in 1836. He ended his days in Venezuela, where he lived on his pension as a retired general.

The Royal Panopticon of Science and Art

The Odeon cinema which stands today on the eastern side of Leicester Square in London was for a short while, from 1854 until 1857, the site of a bizarre and exotic construction in the Saracen style of architecture. It was known as the 'Royal Panopticon of Science and Art'.

The brief career of this institution, intended to popularise the arts and applied sciences, began on 21 February 1850, when the promoter of the idea, Edward Marmaduke Clarke, an Irishman who had previously staged art and science exhibitions in London, obtained a royal charter of incorporation. The company of which he became the managing director was capitalised at £80,000. After launching the company, Clarke looked for suitable premises for his Panopticon. He secured a sixty-year lease for a site on the eastern side of Leicester Square. The construction of the Panopticon itself began in 1851. Clarke was personally responsible for the idea to have the building designed in the Moorish style.

To give its readers an impression of the finished aspect of the building in course of erection, the *Illustrated London News* reported on 31 January 1852 that 'while the erection in question will attempt to convey a model of Moorish grandeur, it will be no servile copy of any existing edifice'. As the architect had pointed out, 'the Saracens had not been in the habit of building Panopticon institutions'! The roof was originally planned in the shape of a big onion dome, whose design had been copied from a Cairo mosque, while the façade was flanked by two tall minarets. In the end, the onion dome became a sixteen-sided low cone, topped by a flat glass skylight, but the minarets remained. The interior of the Panopticon consisted of a vast circular hall, 97 feet in diameter and equally high, surrounded by three galleries in which works of art, industry and science were exhibited to the public. A huge and powerful organ also occupied part of the space in the central hall.

The Royal Panopticon of Science and Art opened to the public on 17 March 1854. Within one month, it attracted over one thousand visitors a day coming to watch the large illuminated fountain in the centre of the rotunda, from which a powerful jet of water would leap up as high as the roof by means of a steam-operated pump. Reviewing the exhibition on 18 March 1854, the *Illustrated London News* commented optimistically that the scheme 'promised much for the popular spread of science in its application to the arts and industry'. In fact, the company collapsed shortly

With its richly engraved borders, depicting symbols representing the various arts and enumerating the names of famous scientists, this share certificate in the Royal Panopticon of Science and Art was registered in 1851 in the name of its originator, Edward Marmaduke Clarke, an Irishman who had obtained a royal charter of incorporation for the company on 21 February 1850. After its initial success, the company collapsed and the premises were offered for sale by auction in 1856.

afterwards, due to poor management and lack of specific purpose in the enterprise. One writer, alluding later to the failure of the Panopticon, attributed it to 'the unnatural alliance of religious profession and commercial enterprise'.

Offered for sale by auction as from August 1856, the premises were acquired by a theatrical promoter for the sum of £9000, whereas, according to contemporary estimates, the cost of building and furnishing the Panopticon had exceeded £80,000. Under its new ownership the building became known as the Alhambra Palace, where circus and music-hall performances used to be staged.

Guide to Prices

Market value of banknotes and bonds illustrated in the text
Prices valid at time of going to press

Item	Value		Page No.
Ming Dynasty Note for 1 kwan, issued in the year 1368 AD	£950	$1,900	12
Hansatsu, 3 momme note of Osaka, 1844	£5	$10	14
Swedish signed banknote, 1666, 10 dalers	£5,000	$10,000	16
German 20, 50 and 100 billion mark notes, 1920's	£1,000	$2,000	18
French 'invasion' money, 5,000 French francs	£1,000	$2,000	19
City of Cologne Municipal External Loan, $1,000, 1925	£5	$10	20
Henry VIII hand signed pay warrant, 1514	£3,000	$6,000	23
Bank of England 'white' note, £1,000	£5,750	$11,500	25
Bank of England 'inscribed' stock, 1834	£20	$40	26
Belgian Banque Nationale 10,000 Franc note, 1929	£175	$350	28
Banque Centrale du Mali, 5,000 Franc note, 1971–1973	£22	$44	30
Czechoslovakian Ministry of Finance, 500 Korun note, 1919	£100	$200	31
Banque du Canada $25 note, 1935	£600	$1,200	32
Icelandic Islands Banki, 10 Kronur, 1920	£250	$500	32
Portuguese Banco de Portugal, 100 MilReis note, 1909	£450	$900	33
Sunderland Bank £5 note, 18– (printers proof)	£175	$350	34
Banco de Espana 1,000 Pesetas, 1895	£1,500	$3,000	34
Hong Kong and Shanghai Banking Corporation, $10 note 1913	£350	$700	35
Waterlow and Sons publicity note	£30	$60	38
Belgian Congo Banque Centrale, 500 Franc note, 1959	£185	$370	38
Swedish Wenersborg Enskilda Banken, 50 Kronor note, 1879	£400	$800	39
Banco de Espana, 100 Pesetas, 1906	£35	$70	40
Cyfarthfa & Hirwain Iron Works, 1 Guinea note, 1825	£200	$400	41
American Chesapeake & Ohio Canal Company, $10 note, 1840	£28	$56	42
Canadian Bank of Commerce, $10 note, 1917	£150	$300	43
Norwegian 'Krigsseddel' note, 100 Kroner, 1944	£850	$1,700	44
'Che' Guevara signed note, 1961	£5	$10	47
New Jersey note, £6, 1776	£50	$100	48
American revolutionary note, 1775	£200	$400	49
US Treasury Warrant, hand signed by Sam Houston, 1861	£350	$700	50
French Revolution, 10,000 Franc note,	£25	$50	51
French Louis XVI 'Royal Assignat', 300 Livres	£650	$1,300	52
Hungarian hand signed note, 50 Dollars	£250	$500	53
Republic of Nicaragua, 50 Dollar note, 1856	£1,500	$3,000	54
Equitable Labour Exchange note, 1832–1834	£30	$60	55
Austrian lottery bond, issued by Austrian Red Cross Company, 1882	£4	$8	56
Compagnie Universelle du Canal Interoceanique de Panama, 500 Franc bearer share	£20	$40	58
Genoa & District Water Works, bond 1913	£30	$60	59
Madeira-Mamoré Railway, bond £100.	£20	$40	60

Item	Value		Page No.
Société Coloniale de Plantations et Cultures à Madagascar, 100 Franc bearer share, 1927	£8	$16	61
Brazilian Railway Company bond	£30	$60	62
Oriental Bank Corporation, share certificate £25, 1853	£25	$50	63
Colquitt Street Tontine share, 1807	£60	$120	64
New South Sea Annuities, 1771	£30	$60	68
The Great Ship Company Ltd, share certificate £1	£20	$40	69
Manchester Exchange share	£10	$20	70
Barcelona Traction, Light & Power Company, bond	£10	$20	71
Ottoman Railway Company, bearer share £20, 1862	£30	$60	72
Herne Bay Pier Company, share certificate No 40, 1833	£70	$140	73
Mission Development Company, cancelled certificate for 100 shares	£5	$10	74
Missouri, Kansas & Texas Railway Company, share certificate, 1887	£95	$190	75
Kreuger & Toll Inc., share certificate, 1928	£6	$12	76
Hongkong & Shanghai Banking Corporation, specimen share	£80	$160	78
Pekin Syndicate Ltd, share warrant 25 Shansi shares, £1 each	£85	$170	81
Shanghai-Hangchow-Ningpo railway, National Government of China 6 per cent loan	£300	$600	83
Hukuang Railways Gold Loan, 1911, £20 bond	£850	$1,700	84
Chinese Government 5 per cent Gold Loan, 1912	£1,200	$2,400	87
Chinese Government Reorganisation Loan, 1913	£115	$230	88
Russian 4 per cent State Loan, bearer bond, 2,000 German Reichsmarks, 1902	£25	$50	91
City of Nicolaef, second issue bond	£300	$600	92
Grand Russian Railway Company 3 per cent loan, bond 625 Roubles	£45	$90	95
Confederate State of America, bond $1,000, 1861	£20	$40	97
Confederate States of America 'Cotton Bond', 1863	£75	$150	98
Accessory Transit Company of Nicaragua, $1,000, 1855	£85	$170	100
Baltimore & Ohio Railroad Company, share certificate 1903	$12	$24	102
Blue Ridge Railroad Company, $1,000 bond, 1869	£60	$120	103
American Express Company, early share, 1857	£325	$650	105
Merchants Union Express Company, unissued certificate	£125	$250	108
Strand Bridge Company, share certificate, 1809	£100	$200	109
Wear Valley Railway, £25 bearer share	£60	$120	111
Dundee, Perth and London Shipping Company, share certificate, 1868	£10	$20	112
State and Government of Poyais, £100 bearer bond, 1823	£85	$170	113
Royal Panopticon of Science and Art, share certificate, 1851	£40	$80	115

117

Dealers, Auction Houses,
Clubs and Magazines
who specialise in Banknotes
and Bonds

Banknote Dealers

M. Ableson
Sandhill House
Templar Place
Leeds 2

W. Barrett
Box 9
Victoria
Montreal H32 2V4
Canada

C. Desai
P.O.Box 106
Rajkot (Gujarat)
India

D. Keable
38 Clyde Road
Croydon
Surrey

W. Mitkoff
P.O.Box 1016
Pittsfield
Massachussetts 01201
USA

Spink and Son Ltd
5–7 King Street
St James's
London SW1Y 6QS

M. Steinberg
P.O. Box 226
Yellow Springs
Ohio 45387
USA

Stanley Gibbons
395 Strand
London WC2R 0LX

T. Uhl
Drawer 1444
Anburndale
Florida 33823
USA

Auction Houses

Stanley Gibbons
395 Strand
London WC2R 0LX

Henry Christensen Inc
P.O.Box 1732
Madison
New Jersey 07940
USA

NASGA
265 Surise Highway Suite
53 Rockville Centre
New York 11570
USA

Club and Magazines

Society of Paper Money
Collectors
C/o Harold Hauser
P.O.Box 150
Glen Ridge
New Jersey 07028
USA

International Bank Note
Society
C/o C. E. Stanier
46 Silhill Hall Road
Solihull
West Midlands
Warwickshire B91 1JU

Bank Note Reporter
P.O.Box 9
Camden
South Carolina 29020
USA

Essay Proof Society
C/o Barbara R. Mueller
225S Fisher Avenue
Jefferson
Wisconsin 53549
USA

Bond Dealers

Belcher Associates
352 Grand Building
London WC2

T. Isler
Edison Strasse 10
CH – 8050
Zurich
Switzerland

F. Kuhlmann
Seiler Strasse 15–17
3000 Hanover 1
West Germany

Spink and Son Ltd
5–7 King Street
St James's
London SW17 6QS

Stanley Gibbons
395 Strand
London WC2R 0LX

F. M. Sutor
Luetzow Strasse 78
5650 Solingen 1
West Germany

R.M. Smythe & Co. Inc.
'Old Securities'
170 Broadway
New York
NY 10038
USA

Clubs

The Bond and Share Society
C/o B. W. Mills
The Treasurer
56 The Avenue
Tadworth
Surrey KT20 5DE